SUPER EASY
BAG
LUNCHES

Recipes and Hundreds of Other
Happy Baggin' It Ideas

Maxine Sprague, BEd.

The Learning Center Press

Box 82016 GMO#2 Heritage Village
Edmonton, Alberta T6J 7E6

SUPER EASY
BAG LUNCHES

© 1999 Maxine Sprague, BEd.

First Printing April 1999

ISBN 0-9691665-2-4

Canadian Cataloguing in Publication Data

Sprague, Maxine
    Super easy bag lunches : recipes and hundreds of other
happy baggin' it ideas

Includes index.
ISBN 0-9691665-2-4

   1. Lunchbox cookery. I. Title. II. Title: Bag lunches.

TX735.S67 1999   641.5'3   C99-900261-9

Printed and Bound in Canada by Hignell Book Printing Limited
Typesetting and Graphics: Microsoft® Publisher 97

To Mom,
Mary K. Black

A terrific lunch maker who rarely
mixed up our sandwiches and who
always heard about it when she did.

As a parent of 3 children, I know
how difficult it is to come up with
refreshing ideas and I've certainly come
to appreciate the 3000 lunches
my mom made for me.

Acknowledgments

Thank you to my husband, Robert, and our children, Jennifer, Cathryn and Cindy, for all your support and encouragement.

Thank you to family and friends for your many ideas which have been an inspiration while writing this book.

Thank you to Alison Craig, B.Sc., R.D. for your contribution to the nutritional information.

About the Author

Maxine Sprague, BEd. is a parent, author and educator. She lives in Edmonton with her husband and three children. Super Easy Bag Lunches is her third book. Her previously published books include Creative Parenting Ideas and Activities and Positive Parenting Strategies. Maxine enjoys doing group presentations and seminars for adults and children. She loves hiking, sewing, gardening, composting, travelling and spending time with her family and friends.

Contents

Introduction

It's 7 AM. You're hurriedly fixing breakfast while hoping for some fresh inspiration to create a fabulous lunch that your children won't trade away for their classmate's junk food.

A variety of gourmet delights wander through your mind when suddenly you snap back to reality. The fridge is empty and the cupboards are stripped down to a few dry crackers. A feeling of despair passes over you as you reach for the peanut butter. You hope the kids won't notice. After all, it's only the third time this week you've sent peanut butter but then, it is only Wednesday. Oh, if you'd only made that dreaded grocery shopping trip. You hurriedly spread the peanut butter and slap the sandwiches together, silently vowing to shape up for tomorrow's lunches.

Did you know that children who take bag lunches will require about 2400 of them during their school years? Multiply that by the diverse tastes of all the bag lunchers in your family and you can see why it takes a lot of energy, planning and effort to come up with nutritious, refreshing ideas day after day and year after year.

Super Easy Bag Lunches is packed full of creative ideas that will inspire you to make terrific bag lunches.

I've included hints and ideas to get your life organized and last minute quick fixes for hurried mornings. I'll share with you easy ways to save time and money and to teach your children to view eating as a positive experience.

It's fun to grow your own food for lunches and I'll show you how to boost your yields and nutritional value through composting. If you enjoy sewing, there's a pattern for making a reuseable lunch bag. For those concerned about our environment, there are ideas for packing a litterless lunch.

To prevent lunches from becoming boring, check out the tips for perking them up; fun foods, riddles and other reproducible lunch box smiles. Nutrition is a lunch time concern, so I've included practical advice from a professional registered dietitian.

If you are out of ideas for school snack days, you'll appreciate the special recipes that travel well and satisfy a roomful of picky eaters.

So there you have it; recipes and so much more. I know you'll find many useful ideas in **Super Easy Bag Lunches** that will have your children saying "Great Lunch today!" Beautiful words to a lunch maker's ears.

Happy Baggin' It!

Lunch Bucket History

In the days of the one room schoolhouse, children carried their lunch in a cloth sack or tin lard pail.

The first commercial metal lunch box was produced by Aladdin® in 1950. It was designed in red or blue and had a 4" decal of "Hopalong Cassidy" centered on the front. Sales from this lunch box were so good that Aladdin® built a new plant and produced a "Tom Corbett Space Cadet" decal box in 1952.

In 1953, the first fully lithographed box was produced by the American Thermos Company®. It was a "Roy Rogers and Dale Evans" box with a full lithograph of their "Double R Bar Ranch". This box sold 2.5 million in it's first year.

Metal lunch boxes began to be banned in 1972 when a group of Florida mothers campaigned against them. They said the kids were using them to hit and cause permanent damage to each other.

Metal lunch boxes were produced in a rectangular box style or a domed shape and usually included a matching thermos. Although over 120 million metal lunch boxes were sold between 1950 and 1970, only about 450 different designs were produced in North America.

Vinyl Lunch boxes were produced in 1959 and by 1970, plastic lunch boxes were outselling metal ones. The last metal lunch box was produced in 1985 by KST®. It was a "Sylvester Stalone Rambo" edition.

Metal and Plastic lunch boxes have become collector's items. The rarity of the box, the condition it is in and the demand for it determine the asking price.

I still have my metal lunch box but it probably wouldn't be a collector's item. The handle was scavenged from someone else's lunch box and is slightly melted so it must have been set too near the wood stove at some point. The outside is a brown texture with a dashed ropelike design around the edge. The inside has been repainted to curb the rust problem from leaky thermoses. It also has a new latch, thanks to my handyman dad, since I like many others suffered the embarrassment of strewing my lunch behind me when the latch sprung open on it's own accord. My children are intrigued by my metal lunch box and wonder how it could have lasted "soooo" long since their vinyl ones give out yearly.

Current lunch boxes come in a variety of sizes, shapes and materials. Some have even returned to the one room school house cloth sack. I've included directions for making one later in the "Perk It Up" section. They won't last as long as my metal lunch box but they're softer and probably won't be banned by concerned mothers.

YOU CAN'T MAKE ME EAT IT

*BUT MOM, I'M SURE THE BROCCOLI SAID,
"PLEASE DON'T EAT ME."*

You Can't Make Me Eat It

When I was growing up, I would hear people say, "You can lead a horse to water but you can't make him drink." That saying reminds me of children's eating habits. You can slave for hours in the kitchen, use your finest place settings, even dine by candlelight but if your child isn't hungry or doesn't like the cuisine, you can't, using reasonable methods, make them eat it.

There are some things you can do to increase the possibility that they will eat what you serve.

 ## Ten Tips for Picky Eaters

1. Offer a wide variety of nutritious food and look at the bigger picture.

Children's eating can be very unpredictable and fluctuate sporadically. They love something one day and hate it the next. They'll be just starving one minute and not hungry a few minutes later. Serving a variety of food and gently encouraging them to eat a balance at every meal will eliminate many mealtime battles. Looking at the bigger picture helps you see that the balance might not come all in one day but generally averages out over several days.

2. Don't force children to eat.

Making food an item of contention between you and your child will leave you on the losing end of the battle. Just how do you force a child to swallow something he doesn't want to? "Open wide for the little birdie" and "Choo, choo, choo, let the train in the tunnel" just don't cut it after the first few months of eating. Children are very adept at finding creative solutions to avoid the dreaded items; hiding them in cheeks, pockets or on a sibling's plate, feeding the pet under the table and threatening to throw up. Now, that's one threat I'd rather not challenge. Put yourself in their position. Would you enjoy someone forcing you to eat something you absolutely detest? It's not a pleasant situation to be in as you may recall from your own childhood.

Telling your children stories of starving children may just be enough motivation to set their minds whirling on creative ways to deliver the string beans and brussel sprouts to those hungry, starving children. Children need to be taught to be thankful they have plenty to eat and to be compassionate and share with others who don't but this information should not be a bargaining chip for mealtime negotiations.

3. Make mealtime a positive experience. ☑

Eating is not a competitive event with food as the reward. Setting dessert up as the prize for eating the rest of the meal elevates high fat, overly sweet food to a position of unearned importance, creating habits of overeating and craving for unhealthy foods. Keeping positive and negative pressure to a minimum where food is involved makes for a relaxed eating atmosphere. Keep informed about your child's lunch room atmosphere at school. A stressful school lunch time can seriously affect a child's ability to function well at school.

4. Teach children to view food as nourishment for active, healthy bodies.

Educate your child through reading books and discussing how their bodies work. Understanding why their bodies need fuel and what foods provide them with the best fuel will help them make wiser food choices.

5. Stock up on nutrient rich foods.

The foods you have readily available in your home will influence your children's diet and eating style. Keep moderation and variety in mind when you stock your food shelves.

6. Involve your children in the planning, shopping, growing and preparation of food.

Encouraging your child to make decisions about what to serve and how to eat encourages independent thinking skills and responsible decision making. The skills involved in food preparation will be useful for a lifetime. Teaching them to take small portions and add a little more if they are still hungry helps prevent food wasting.

7. Offer healthy between meal snacks for days when they're absolutely famished and couldn't possibly wait until the next meal.

8. Be aware of other influences such as peer pressure and advertising.

Foods that are totally yuck one week may be just the coolest next. Food should not be in your Top 10 List of Peer Issues that are worth arguing about. Save your breath for more critical peer problems. Educating children about the powerful medium of advertising at a very young age will help them make wiser decisions and become more immune to it's influence.

9. Set a positive example.

Abraham Lincoln is credited with saying that "the only way to bring up a child in the way he should go, is to travel that way yourself". Forcing your child to finish that one last bite encourages poor eating habits. Look at it this way, the bite is gone whether it travels your child's digestive tract or makes an early exit to the compost bucket. It is more harmful to encourage overeating than to feed your compost pile. Eat when you're hungry, quit when you're full is good advice.

10. Serve food children enjoy.

Foods come in a variety of textures, temperatures, flavors and combinations. Children are unique individuals and some are more sensitive to these variations in foods while others will eat almost anything. With the wide variety of foods available, there are many choices that will satisfy both nutrition and taste. Be sensitive to your child, serve foods they enjoy along with foods that you encourage them to experience.

Keeping your child's likes and dislikes in mind, serving child-size portions and encouraging them to sample new foods will help create a positive attitude toward food and eating. A significant portion of our lives revolves around food; planning, growing, shopping, preparing, serving, eating and cleaning up afterwards. To make healthy eating a positive experience for our families is a gift that will bring shared pleasure and endure for a lifetime.

Easy to Eat Lunches

Sometimes lunch foods go uneaten because children don't want to be bothered peeling something you've packed or items are too messy to eat.

- Make oranges easier to eat by cutting slits so the wedges of skin peel away easily.
- Precut fruit and put it in a plastic container with a snap lid. Include a spoon to eat it with.
- To prevent icing from sticking to the container, cut the bottom half off the piece of cake and place it on top so the icing is sandwiched between the layers.
- Cut a small slit near the stem of the banana so the skin peels away easily.

GET IT TOGETHER

I AM ORGANIZED, I JUST CAN'T FIND ANYTHING IN MY PILING SYSTEM.

Get It Together

There is nothing worse than a messy kitchen, empty fridge and bare cupboards when you have to make lunches. One of the keys to turn lunch making into an enjoyable task, or should I say tolerable task, is to get organized. This will take time and effort in the beginning but it's well worth the trouble.

When I was younger, my mom always said she wouldn't dare open a closet when I had my own home because she might be crushed in the avalanche. My room cleaning methods back then involved shoving everything in the closet and quickly closing the door before it all fell out.

Over the years and several moves with a family of five, I've had to learn how to organize not only for my own safety and sanity but also to set an example for my children.

Maybe you were born organized and are the envy of all your friends. If so, you can skip this chapter. On the other hand, if you've had to learn like I did and you're still struggling to get organized, keep reading for some practical help.

Organizing Your Home

1. Quit making excuses about your disorganized state and take action to change it.

2. Dejunk – Give it up.

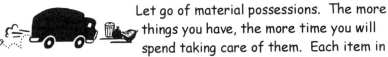

Let go of material possessions. The more things you have, the more time you will spend taking care of them. Each item in your home should have a purpose; either it's useful or it's genuinely attractive as a display item. For several years, I made and sold woodworking and folk art painting. Many friends have commented how little of it I have in my home. I always tell them, tongue in cheek, " I don't mind getting paid to clutter other people's homes but I don't enjoy wasting time dusting my own clutter".

3. Give everything a place and put it back when you're done with it.

Avoid the "I'll just put it here for now" syndrome. Those "here for nows" can build up at an incredible pace. If you're afraid to move things because of an avalanche hazard, it's time to get rid of your "here for now" piling system and adopt a new system; "a place for everything and everything in it's place". If you have problems getting your children to put things in their place, gather everything that's left lying around into a large Lost and Found Box. When your child complains about a missing item, tell them to search the box. Have them leave cash or a favorite toy or CD as a deposit on borrowed items. You'll return theirs when they return yours. Fair enough.

4. Set a limit on the number of items of a particular kind that you want to store.

For example, no more than 6 plastic pails, 4 empty boxes, 10 plastic food containers or 2 works of children's art per year.

5. Don't be a storage company for others.

If they don't want it bad enough to store it themselves, why would you want to store it for them? Which reminds me. I better get that ping pong table back before my sister reads this. It was good of her to store it all these years.

6. Get your children to care for their own clutter.

Encourage them to be more selective about what they wish to keep by having them store and care for their own things. Helping them go through their keepsakes at regular intervals, tossing items that are no longer significant, will teach them to be responsible for their own clutter. Confining keepsakes to one container will also require them to discard items so they can add something new.

7. Organize your workspace.

All items used daily should be stored in easy to reach places near the location they will be used. Items that are used once or twice a year can be stored in harder to reach places or another area of the house. Set up a baking center where all utensils and supplies are within easy reach. Use drawer dividers so everything isn't in a tangled heap. If you haven't used an item in the last year, give it away or throw it out. Stores are full of time saving gadgets and appliances that take up valuable space, don't work as advertised or take so long to clean you use up all the time you saved in the first place.

8. Clean as you go.

Wipe up spills when they happen rather than waiting for a major cleaning day. Filling the sink with sudsy water before you start baking will also make clean up a breeze. If something boils over, clean the burner when you do the dishes that same day.

 Wipe fridge shelves just before you need to grocery shop. Move everything to the left side and wipe the right. Then, move it all right to wipe the left. A quick wipe around the door seals and you're done.

9. Recruit Help.

Teach your children to clean up after themselves. If you get something out, put it away. If you dirty something, clean it. Have a cleaning day and post the jobs on a sign up sheet. Children usually work better if they have some say in what they are doing. Developing self discipline and an attitude of team work in your children is well worth the effort.

Organize Your Schedule

Finding a system that works for you is the key to organizing your day. Some form of day timer is a must for everyone. I like to use a full size binder with pages that show a full week at a time. I design the pages on the computer so I can customize them to fit my needs. I put everything in my day timer including scheduled times for laundry and watering plants. I put a small circle in front of each item so I can check it off when I have completed it. It's easy to look back over the week and see items that were not completed and move them to another day.

Another helpful tool is a large wipe off calendar on the fridge or a bulletin board. Using different colored ink for each family member helps keep the schedules sorted out. Check your day timer and calendar first thing in the morning and last thing at night to refresh your memory.

Giving each child their own calendar or agenda book encourages them to be responsible for their own schedules.

In the evening, check that homework has been completed and put in backpacks, along with other necessary items.

 Give children their own alarm clocks. Each child can wake up according to the amount of time they require to get ready to go.

Get a head start on the morning rush by getting up at least half an hour before everyone else. Relax over breakfast, read the paper or plan the day's schedule and you'll be better prepared to handle the day ahead.

Check the weather and lay out clothes the night before so there is less decision making in the morning.

If family members share a bathroom, put a clock in the bathroom and set up a schedule. No more yelling, "What time is it?" or running out to check the time.

Learn to say NO! Over scheduling your family with sports, lessons and other activities will leave you all tired and stressed. Ask yourself these questions before signing up for any activity.

1. Do I have adequate time in my schedule to add this activity?

2. Are my children really interested in this activity or am I pushing them into something I wished I had been able to do as a child?

3. Am I really interested in doing this or do I feel pressured by others to participate?

4. Do those organizing the activity truly care about the welfare of my child or is profit and bottom line their motive?

5. Do I feel completely confident leaving my children alone with these people? Will they take care of my child with as much love and concern as I would?

6. Would the time and money be better spent doing something together as a family?

Children are in our care for such a short time, we really need to use those years to help them grow up to be self-disciplined, independent and happy adults. Keeping children on the run and constantly entertained prevents them from developing their minds through creative play and time spent day dreaming, planning, analyzing and refreshing their whole selves.

When it comes to making decisions about what activities and responsibilities to take on, "moderation in all things" has served me well. The little word NO has also been a sanity saver. Life is just too short to spend it doing things you can't really put your heart into or rushing here and there with no real purpose.

Organize Your Shopping

Fifty or Sixty years ago, parents had limited choices when it came to shopping. Today, we are bombarded with glitzy ads, sale of the century signs, coupons, discounts, rebates, don't pay until the year something or other, giant discount warehouse stores, one stop supermarket shopping, gigantic malls, info-mercials, 1-800-24 hr. mail order, easy credit and world wide internet access. Keeping control of your spending habits and teaching children how to manage money are necessary life skills in today's world.

Grocery items are one area of your budget where you can make considerable savings with very little effort using good shopping habits and commonsense. This is especially true when it comes to packed lunches. Store shelves are bulging with an enormous variety of costly, prepackaged lunch and snack foods aimed at capturing the dollars of busy parents. Clever marketing strategies, phenomenal advertising budgets and attractive packaging are used to target your children so they will talk you into buying them the latest and greatest lunch snack. Not only are these individually packaged snacks expensive, many of them are nutritionally deficient and add excessive amounts of fat, salt, sugar and chemical additives to your youngster's diet.

Making wise shopping decisions is an excellent way to save money. Here are some tips that will help make shopping for groceries a money saving adventure.

1. Teach children money saving strategies. Talk about advertising, using teachable moments not lecture style.

2. Set a wise-consumer example for your children by reading labels, comparing prices and sticking to a budget.

3. Narrow choices for children by having them select between two cereals rather than asking which cereal they would like.

4. Set up a shopping budget and use a pocket calculator to keep track of totals as you shop.

5. Limit prepackaged lunch box snacks to one or two per week.

6. Compare brands and try using cheaper brands to see if the quality is the same or close enough to justify the savings.

7. Know your prices. Sales can be deceiving and difficult to compare when the size of the product varies. Keep a notebook of prices on frequently purchased products and carry a calculator so you can quickly compare. Dividing your notebook by type of product such as dairy, meat, produce, etc. or listing products in alphabetical order will make looking them up much easier. An oversized address book would work well for this.

8. Don't shop when the stores are busy so you have plenty of time to compare prices and save money. Shopping when you're hungry isn't a good idea either. If you have problems resisting your children's wants, shop without them if possible. Add just one or two over packaged, overpriced items to your cart and you could literally "eat up" all your savings in a matter of minutes.

9. Prepare a comprehensive shopping list that includes all items you need to help you avoid impulse buys and unplanned shopping trips. How many cashiers have keyed in $100.00 of purchases and heard the customer remark, "I only stopped by for a couple of items."?   Preparing a master list of items you always buy allows you to tick off just what you need when you notice you're running low. Designing the list according to your favorite store's floor plan makes shopping easier.

10. Check the Best Before Dates to be sure you are getting the freshest product.

11. Watch at the checkout as cashiers sometimes make errors or the computer may not have had a sale price programmed into it. Catching the error when it happens makes fixing it easier than if you discover it later at home.

12. When buying cuts of meat, consider the cost per serving rather than price per kilogram. Lower priced meat may not serve as many because of wasted fat and bones and could end up costing more per serving.

13. Use a calculator or shelf labels to compare unit pricing. Divide the total cost by the number of grams to get the cost/gram. This will allow you to easily compare brands and different sized containers.

14. Look high and low. The most expensive brands are often placed in the most convenient location. Grocery stores are designed to sell you products with clever marketing strategies like routing you past inviting displays, serving samples, putting an odd number of aisles so you have to go past items twice, using signs that appear to be sales but are regular prices and setting limits on the number of items at a certain price or buy 2 and get a cheaper price. Make sure you buy the items you want rather than the ones they want to sell you.

15. Coupons are a nuisance but the savings can be significant if you use them only for items you would normally purchase. Make sure you check that an item with a coupon is actually cheaper than a comparable item without a coupon. You can also check if your store accepts competitor's coupons. Running to several stores to save a few cents at each usually doesn't pay off because of the extra time and gas consumed. Circling or highlighting the expiry date on the coupon will alert you to use them before they expire.

16.   Buy in season and freeze or can for later use. Buy bulk when items are on sale, if you have available storage space.

17.   Plan a major, comprehensive shopping trip once a month. Stock up on non-perishables and then make short weekly trips for perishables. Many supermarkets put perishables around the outside so you can easily zip down the fresh fruits and vegetables aisle and breeze back up the dairy aisle. Reading store flyers will allow you to take advantage of sale items which you can quickly pick up on these weekly trips. Remember, the less time you spend in the store, the less money you are likely to spend.

BEAT THE
CLOCK

I'VE COME TO THE CONCLUSION THAT I'D HAVE EVERYTHING
DONE ON TIME IF THE CLOCK WASN'T SO FAST.

Beat the Clock

Buying food and preparing lunches uses up a lot of valuable time. Here are some tips to help save time when making lunches.

1. Make up a quantity of sandwiches at one time and freeze them. Hamburger, turkey, chicken, tuna, beef, ham, jam and peanut butter all freeze well. Frozen sandwiches will help keep your child's lunch cold and will be thawed by lunch time. Package lettuce, tomato, cucumber and other garnishes separately to be added just before eating.

2. Save the leftover packets of ketchup, dips and sauces from take out food to put in lunches.

3. Making your own convenience foods and storing them in the freezer saves having to buy expensive, over preserved, prepackaged foods and making last minute plans to eat out or
 order in. Spend a few minutes mixing several batches of dry ingredients for a favorite loaf, cake or muffins and you'll have your own prepackaged mixes. Just add the wet ingredients and bake.

4. Buy large quantities of deli meat when they are on sale and get them sliced thinly. Lay individual sandwich sized portions on cookie sheets and freeze. When frozen, put them all in a freezer container. It's quick and easy to remove just the amount you need and pack along with bread for a sandwich. You can save even more by thinly slicing your own meat from left overs such as roast beef, pork, chicken and turkey.

5. Have a major baking day when you cook up large quantities to freeze for later use. Inviting a friend to spend the day cooking with you or involving the kids is a great way to turn a chore into an anticipated event.

6. Chop leftover beef, ham, pork, chicken or turkey and freeze for quick sandwiches, taco fillings, salads, soups and stews.

7. Grate quantities of cheese and freeze. It's easy to take a small amount out to put in a sandwich or taco or use as a topping for pizza, cheese bread or casseroles.

8. Leftovers from dishes such as lasagne can be frozen in individual serving portions which can be quickly reheated and packed in a thermos. Make up the leftovers from meals such as tacos or hot dogs and freeze immediately. They are easy to send in lunches or reheat for after school snacks.

9. Make a list of sandwiches and other items each child likes so you can consult it if you run out of ideas. Get your child to make a list of things he would like to have in his lunch. Talk about what others bring in their lunches that he finds appealing.

10. Share lunchmaking with a friend. She makes your child's lunch every other day or for a week at a time and vice versa.

11. Find out how much time your children are allowed for eating their lunches and include foods that can be eaten in that amount of time. Hard, crunchy foods take longer to chew. Having too many of these items in a lunch requires too much time to eat them, especially if children are excited to get out and play with their friends.

Stock the Shelves

Having a well stocked cupboard, fridge and freezer will make lunch preparation so much easier. You might include some of the following when you stock up.

Cupboard

- Flour
- Baking Powder
- Baking Soda
- Corn Starch
- Corn Meal
- Vanilla
- Cream of Tarter
- Crackers
- Pasta
- Rice
- Potatoes
- Onions
- Vegetable oil
- Vinegar
- Salt
- Pepper
- Favorite Spices such as paprika, chili powder, basil, oregano, parsley, thyme, garlic, nutmeg, cinnamon, bay leaves, sage, ginger.
- Canned Goods such as tomatoes, tomato paste, pizza and pasta sauce, soups, tuna, salmon, vegetables.

Fridge

- Milk
- Butter
- Eggs
- Cheese
- Bread
- Mayonnaise
- Ketchup
- Mustard
- Salad Dressing
- Vegetables/Fruits
- Peanut Butter

Freezer

- Chicken, Vegetable and Beef Broths
- Meats
- Vegetables
- Frozen Juices
- Cookie Dough
- Pizza
- Bread & Buns

101 Pack and Run Items

When you are pressed for time, it can be hard to think of things to pack into a lunch bag. The following table contains a list of basic foods you can quickly grab and run.

Fruit	Vegetables	Protein	Breads
Bananas	Tomatoes	Boiled Egg	Dry Cereal
Pears	Carrots	Mini Meatballs	Toast
Apples	Celery	Chicken	Pasta
Oranges	Cauliflower	Roast Beef	Bagel
Frozen Fruit	Broccoli	Sliced Pork Chop	Teething Biscuits
Fruit Cocktail	Cherry Tomatoes	Pepperoni Sticks	Graham Crackers
Strawberries	Lettuce	Turkey	Rice
Blueberries	Peas	Spareribs	Cinnamon Buns
Raspberries	Baked Beans	Egg Salad	Zwieback
Cherries	Corn	Chicken Salad	Soda Crackers
Grapes	Pea Pods	Tuna	Pretzels
Dried Fruit	Baby Corn	Salmon	Pizza
Prunes	Cabbage	Ham	Muffins
Nectarines	Potatoes	Peanuts	Bread Sticks
Apricots	Kohlrabi	Beef Jerky	Pancakes
Fruit Leather	Mushrooms	Bacon	Waffles

Fruit	Vegetables	Protein	Breads
Cantaloupe	Radishes	Hot Dogs	Biscuits
Watermelon	Cucumber		Cornbread
Peaches	Onions		Raisin Bread
Canned Fruit	Green Beans		Rice Cakes
Avocado	Turnip		English Muffin
Plums	Zucchini		

Dairy

Cheese	Yogurt	Chocolate Milk	Cottage Cheese
Milk			

Extras

Pickles	Raisins	Pudding	Cupcakes
Potato Chips	Taco Chips	Fruit Snacks	Pretzels
Cookies	Popcorn	Cream Cheese	Mustard
Olives	Ketchup		

KICKSTART THE DAY

WHY DOES BREAKFAST HAVE TO COME SO EARLY IN THE DAY.

Kickstart the Day

Breakfast is an important meal to help kick start your day. In many schools, subjects such as Math and Language Arts are scheduled in the morning when children are fresh and eager to learn. Hungry kids tend to be more tired and lack the concentration skills and attention spans of their well fed classmates. Encourage your children to eat a good breakfast.

When it comes to breakfast, think variety. If your child insists on eating the same thing every morning, try offering something extra such as fruit, cheese slices, juice, etc. served on a colorful dish or in an unusual shape. If the food looks attractive, your child might be enticed into trying a few nibbles.

Think nutrition, not tradition. See if your kids know what two things you can't eat for Breakfast? The answer is Lunch and Dinner. Groan. For a change of pace, serve some lunch and dinner foods for breakfast. Vegetable sticks and dip or leftover pizza might be just the food to satisfy your child's breakfast appetite. Remember, any food can be served at any meal.

In a morning rush? Get an early start by setting the table and checking the fridge for milk and juice the night before. Store breakfast items within children's reach so they can make their own.

Breakfast should be easy to prepare, quick to eat and nutritious. Be aware of individual preferences. Some kids don't feel hungry right away and may require a mid-morning snack if allowed at recess.

French Toast

Crack an Egg on a plate. Stir to mix. Coat both sides of a slice of Bread with the Egg. Toast on a hot, greased griddle. Turn to brown and cook on both sides. Serve with Butter, Jelly or Syrup.

Cinnamon Toast

Mix 3 T. Sugar and 1 tsp. Cinnamon in an empty salt shaker. Butter toasted bread and shake on the Cinnamon/Sugar mixture.

Porridge

Boil   2 Cups Water with 1/4 tsp. salt

Add   1 C. Rolled Oats

Cook 1 minute, stirring constantly. Reduce heat. Cover. Cook 15 min. Add Milk, Brown Sugar, Cinnamon, Raisins, Honey, Apples, Blueberries or other Fruit.

Toad in a Hole

Use a cookie cutter to cut a hole in the center of a slice of bread. Place bread on a lightly greased skillet and break an egg into the hole. Cook and serve.

SUPER BREAKFAST ITEMS

Mix and match these items to design a balanced breakfast.

blender drinks	eggs
pizza	rice pudding
muffin	toast
cheese	fruit custard
yogurt	soup
bagels	crackers
cinnamon buns	leftovers
cheesebread	grilled cheese
pancakes	milkshake
waffles	fruitshake
scones	macaroni & cheese
biscuits	cinnamon toast
breadsticks	hot chocolate
pretzels	fruit salad
french toast	applesauce
porridge	tacos

RECRUIT
THE TROOPS

*O.K. IT'S FAMILY FUN TIME! LET'S GET THOSE
BAG LUNCHES MADE.*

Recruit the Troops

Cooking with your children is a great way to involve them in the process of decision making and taking responsibility for themselves. Cooking also helps them develop a sense of accomplishment, practice language and math skills and gives them an opportunity to share their creations with others. As a bonus, children are more likely to eat foods they've prepared themselves.

Cooking is a practical life skill and will benefit your children for many years to come. Your efforts will be rewarded when they become skilled enough to prepare a meal on their own, giving you a day off. Wow! Every parent's dream.

Cooking is a fun educational experience. Without even realizing it, children learn about important concepts such as volume, fractions, measurement, chemical reactions, temperature and counting. They also practice language skills by reading and interpreting printed recipes. Cooking is an opportunity to teach nutrition. Children are often surprised to find how much sugar is used to make a batch of cookies or brownies or how much fat is in pie crust and biscuits.

Besides the life skills and educational benefits, cooking is just plain fun and most kids, if given the opportunity, love to cook. It's mud pies for real and the best part is you get to eat them.

Start a recipe file for your children, either on cards or in a ring binder. I like to use magnetic type photo album pages or plastic sleeves to hold my recipes. They are easy to wipe clean. On the other hand, I don't mind a few splotches on my cookbooks. It gives them a certain authenticity. Like I told my sister when she lamented about a spill on the cover of one of her favorite recipe books, "Hey, It's a bonus. This cookbook comes with free product samples."

Use the following ideas to make cooking with your kids a positive learning experience.

1. Plan Ahead

Choose a time when you will be relaxed and not distracted by other interruptions. Easier said than done, I know. Beginning cooks need lots of patience and time to learn by doing things for themselves. A relaxed pace will help you resist grabbing the utensils to do it yourself.

2. Supervise

Have an adult nearby to help with sharp utensils, electric appliances and the stove.

3. Prepare

Wear an apron or old clothes. Tie back long hair, roll up long sleeves and remove jewelry. Wash hands well before and during if you lick your fingers or after handling foods such as raw meat. Fill the sink with soapy water before you begin so it will be easy to wipe up the inevitable messes that cooking brings.

4. Organize

Read the entire recipe and gather ingredients and utensils
before you begin. If you put each ingredient
away as you use it, it will be easy to tell what
you have already put in, if you get interrupted in
the middle of the recipe.

5. Safety First

Turn pot handles inward away from other burners so they don't
overheat or get knocked off the stove. Never reach across
burners or pots that are hot. Use pot holders or oven mitts for
handling hot utensils. Never use wet cloths as steam will form
and burn you. Be careful with electric cords. Use dry hands to
unplug them and make sure they aren't laying across a stove
burner or dangling onto the floor. Have a tray or rack handy to
set items on for cooling. Double check that you have turned all
appliances off when finished cooking. Get cooking and have fun.

Friday is Gum Day
*To save constant pestering to buy junk food and chewing
gum, we chose Friday as treat day. The kids buy something
of their choice on Fridays. If they ask for something on
another day, I just say, "Friday is Gum Day." My youngest
daughter grew up with "Friday Gum Days" and I didn't
realize she thought it was a universal concept until one day,
when she was 4, she wondered what kind of gum her friend
Alison would be having. When asked how she knew Alison
would be having gum that day, she replied, "Well, it's Friday
and Friday is Gum Day." Although we make exceptions,
our Friday Gum Day has been a useful way to limit junk
food. The thought of losing gum day for that week is
enough motivation to discourage pestering.*

FOOD SAFE ZONE

HONEST MOM, I AM BEING CAREFUL.

Food Safe Zone

Packed lunches are often unrefrigerated for several hours before being eaten so it is important to take precautions to insure the food will be safe to eat.

1. Storage

When buying perishable foods, take them home and refrigerate them immediately. Take your picnic cooler along when you grocery shop. In summer, it will keep perishables cool. In winter, it will protect fresh produce and dairy items from freezing. Place perishables near the back of the fridge where the temperature is less likely to fluctuate.

2. Handling

Cleanliness is extremely important when handling food. Thoroughly wash hands, work surfaces and all equipment before preparing lunches. Be careful not to allow juices from raw meat to get onto other foods or surfaces where food may be placed. Use separate utensils, cutting boards and containers for fresh foods and those that must be cooked. Lunch containers should be washed daily in hot, sudsy water. Return all food to the fridge as soon as possible as disease causing bacteria can multiply rapidly at room temperature. Prepare lunches just prior to leaving or refrigerate until you're ready to leave.

3. Cooking

Meat, poultry and eggs should be thoroughly cooked
to kill harmful bacteria. Don't replace cooked
meat on the plate that held the raw meat or use
utensils that have been used on raw meats until
they have been thoroughly washed.

4. Chemical Contaminants

Many potentially harmful chemicals are used on food crops to
deter pests and diseases and to prevent spoilage during storage
and transportation. You can minimize exposure to these
chemicals by:

- thoroughly washing, scrubbing and rinsing fruits and
  vegetables to reduce surface contamination.

- peeling the outer layers of leaves or skin.

- buying locally grown, inseason produce. Farmer's markets are
  a great place to shop and it's easy to find out how the food
  has been grown and handled because many of the vendors are
  selling their own produce. Out of season foods that have
  been stored and transported long distances are more likely to
  be treated with chemicals because of pest and spoilage
  problems.

- growing your own chemical free garden crops
  and raising animals for meat and eggs.

- purchasing certified organically grown produce and meats.
  Interpretations of the word organic vary and it may take a
  little research to find a reputable source.

5. Keep Informed

Information regarding food safety is readily available. Keeping yourself informed is the best way to make decisions to protect you and your family from food related illness and disease. It is also important to educate your children about possible food illnesses and tell them what lunchbag foods should be eaten at lunchtime and not saved for later as they might spoil.

6. Avoid Choking Hazards

Certain foods pose a choking hazard for young children. These include hard candies, nuts, seeds, caramels, toffee, jellybeans, gumdrops, popcorn and chewing gum. It is best to avoid serving these foods to children under 4 years old. Other foods which should be modified before serving to young children include hard fruit and vegetables (remove pits, slice, shred, grate or chop finely), peanut butter (thin layer only), hot dogs (slice lengthwise) and fish (remove bones). Be careful when using toothpicks, skewers or pointed sticks in foods. Have children sit quietly and supervise them while eating.

7. Hot and Cold

Keep hot foods hot and cold foods cold. Some foods, such as mayonnaise, are more prone to spoilage and need to be handled carefully to prevent food related illnesses. Pre-heat or pre-chill a thermos with water before packing it. Use freezy packs to keep the lunch cold. You can also freeze several centimeters of juice or milk in the bottom of a reusable container. Top up the container before packing it in the lunch. Another way to keep a lunch cold is to pack frozen items such as grapes, blueberries and sandwiches.

GET
GROWING
WITH GOLD

ONLY A GREEN THUMB WOULD CALL THIS GOLD.

Get Growing with Gold

Children love to grow food of their own and gardening is a fun way to spend time with them. Growing a garden is a great way to teach kids about nature and nutrition. Planting tiny seeds and watching them grow into food you can eat is a miraculous experience, no matter how many gardens you've grown. As a bonus, children are usually more willing to try different food if they have grown and prepared it themselves.

Children enjoy having their own special area for a garden. Part of your garden can be marked off or a small part of a flower garden could be used. Your choice of plants will depend on the space you have available as well as the climate zone you live in. If you have room, plant strawberries, raspberries and other fruiting plants as well.

I like to plant my garden using the bed method which works well in a small area. The soil in the beds heats up quickly and the closely spaced plants choke out weeds and help conserve moisture. I also plant vegetables in among the flower garden. The extra foliage adds color and interest to the flower beds.

If you are new to gardening, neighbors who garden are a great source of help. They have the experience to know what grows well in your area and are usually happy to share their knowledge and expertise. Local garden centers are another excellent source of information. Most libraries have extensive collections of gardening books written for children and adults.

Gardening is a peaceful, close to nature experience that is truly beneficial to our mental and physical health. Gardening will teach your children that hard work and patience pay off. A garden can be an oasis away from the hustle and bustle of the outside world. So, grab your kids, your tools and seeds and get growing. They'll love you for it and you'll all be healthier.

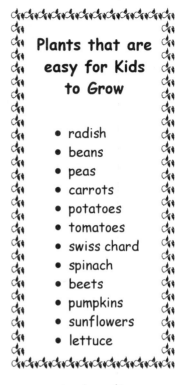

Plants that are easy for Kids to Grow

- radish
- beans
- peas
- carrots
- potatoes
- tomatoes
- swiss chard
- spinach
- beets
- pumpkins
- sunflowers
- lettuce

Gardener's Gold

Did you know you could make gold in your own backyard? O.K. It's not real gold, but compost is called "gardener's gold" because it's so beneficial to your garden and it's completely cost free. My middle daughter says nothing in life is free. I'll correct myself and say that gardener's gold costs only time and a little extra work but it's well worth it.

Composting is nature's way of breaking down the energy and nutrients in organic matter so they can be used again. You can take advantage of this natural process and make it work quickly for you.

Finished compost can be used in your flower beds, vegetable gardens, potted containers and in the bottom of the hole when setting out bedding plants or shrubs.

Four Easy Steps to Finished Compost

 Build a compost container from heavy mesh wire bent in a circular shape. I use stucco wire as it is easy to bend and cut and it holds it's shape well. A container can also be built from wood.

 Layer organic material in a ratio of 2 parts brown, dry material such as dried leaves to 1 part fresh material such as kitchen scraps.

 Keep the pile as moist as a rung out sponge. Add a shovelful of dirt to introduce the organisms that multiply quickly and break down the organic matter. Turn and mix the pile every few weeks.

 When the container is full, start a new pile. The compost is finished when it is dark, crumbly and has a nice earthy smell. Sift out any larger chunks and throw them on the new pile.

Children enjoy composting and are amazed at how nature works to keep recycling nutrients. How wasteful to send these essential life elements to a landfill to be locked away for hundreds of years when you can recycle them in your own backyard. Keeping a compost bucket in your sink cupboard makes it easy to collect household scraps. A trip to the compost pile is a great chore for your kids.

If you need some extra help getting started, ask a friend who composts and consult the library, garden centers, bookstores or your local recycling council for helpful books and literature. It really is very easy and a fun activity to do with your kids while teaching them to take care of the earth around them.

PERK
IT UP

Lunch Bag Smiles

When my children were small, I heard about a neat way to explain love to them using the word picture of a "Love Bucket". We all have our own personal Love Buckets that can be filled to any level just like a bucket of water. We feel best when our Love Buckets are full. Throughout the day, our Love Buckets get jostled and they slop and splash and sometimes even get kicked over. We can fill each other's Love Buckets with acts of kindness, hugs, special privileges, words of appreciation and time spent together. Lunch Bag Smiles, such as an inexpensive treat, fun food or a note are easy ways to fill your children's Love Buckets. You don't have to include something every day and in fact it will be more special if it's an unexpected surprise.

Say "I Love You".

Ask friends who speak a foreign language to tell you the pronunciation and spelling for "I Love You" in their language. Write it to your children and see if they can figure out what language it is.

French	Je t'aime	(ZHE TEM)
German	Ich liebe dich	(ICH LEEBE DICH)
Spanish	Te amo	(TAY AHMO)
Swedish	Jag älskar dig	(YOG ELSKAR DAY)

Memory Bonds

A day at school can be a very long time for young children. Help them feel more secure by creating a memory bond. Select a time when you will think of each other. You might choose morning break, lunch time or snack time. Stress that they don't have to worry if they forget because another chance will come. Tell your child to think of you and how much you love them. When you think of your child, whisper "I Love You" or think of some characteristic they have that you admire. Your child will be comforted to know you are thinking of them. As your children grow older and stormy times develop in your relationship, the memory bond will be an opportunity for both of you to think of each other in a positive way.

Lunch Bag Treats

- stickers
- funky pencils
- jazzy pens
- erasers
- rulers
- shaped notepads
- garage sale finds
- hair accessories
- small toys
- colorful napkins
- unusual eating utensils such as chopsticks or measuring spoons
- newspaper or magazine pictures or articles
- interesting facts about an animal, person, nature

- reminders about after school plans.
- interesting stories from your school days
- riddle or joke
- poem
- short story
- interesting shaped rock, leaf, pinecone or stick
- something to add to their personal collection such as a rock, bottle cap or dinosaur
- Thankyou Note for something they've done
- Congratulations Note for achievements

Pet Smiles

Reproduce these, paste to the back of a picture of your pet and put the picture in your child's lunch .

Dear _____

I wish I was eating your lunch today instead of dry old cat food.

Love,

Dear _____

I wish I was eating your lunch today instead of this dry old dog food.

Love,

Dear _____

I wish I was eating your lunch today instead of

_____.

Love,

Lunch Bag Notes

Reproduce these Lunch Bag Notes, fill in the details and put them in your child's lunch.

CONGRATULATIONS ON:

WOW

Reward:

Love,

Thankyou for making your bed all week. Your reward is

_____

_____.

Love,

Grandma and Grandpa went to school everyday by _____

_____ .

I went to school _____

_____ .

Love,

More Lunch Bag Notes

Reproduce these Lunch Bag Notes, fill in the details and put them in your child's lunch.

When I went to school, something really exciting happened to me. Can you guess what it could be? Read about it on the back of this note. When you get home, tell me about something exciting that happened to you today.

Love,

DON'T FORGET

Please remember to:

Love,

THANKYOU

I really appreciated

Love,

Alphabet Smiles

Using alphabet letters to write notes or writing the notes in different shapes can be lots of fun. Here are some you could reproduce or think up your own.

Some children find it bothers them when classmates find out about their lunchkit notes. Children may tease because of jealousy or unkindness. Be sensitive to your child. I have written really tiny notes in a special spot on my older child's paper lunch bag since Junior High. The middle one doesn't want any notes and the younger one is the envy of all her friends because she gets notes. They all want to read them.

Poetry Smiles

Poems can be a fun way to express your feelings about your child. Use the following to get creative and write your own poetry

Write an Acrostic
Poem using the
letters of your
child's name.

Kind

Artistic

Radiant

Irresistible

Write a Cinquain Poem using the following format.

Line 1 - Name Something

Line 2 - 2 words that describe it

Line 3 - 3 things it does

Line 4 - 4 words telling how you feel about it

Line 5 - Give another name to it

Emily
Grade Three Girl
Runs, Jumps, Laughs
How I Love You
Sweet Heart

Kyle
Tall, Blonde
Quiet, Happy, Kind
You make me smile
Son

You can write on napkins, used greeting cards, shaped notepads, sticky notes, beautiful stationery, computer generated cards, your business card, a photograph, or a receipt from a special meal. Use your imagination.

Mini-Book Smiles

It's simple to make a small booklet and write a whole book of wonderful things to your child. Use the pattern below to fold a sheet of paper into a booklet and get writing. Write it all at once or use it as an ongoing project by writing a new page in it each day or encouraging your child to write back to you.

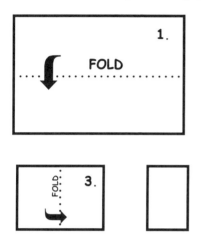

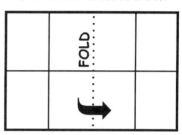

4. UNFOLD AND REFOLD AS SHOWN

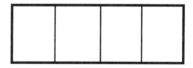

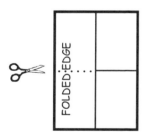

5. CUT BOTH LAYERS AT THE FOLDED EDGE ON THE DOTTED LINE SHOWN BELOW. UNFOLD.

6. REFOLD THE OPPOSITE WAY

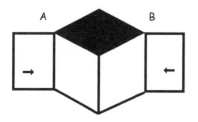

8. NOW GET WRITING!

7. PUSH IN UNTIL POINT **A & B** TOUCH

A SPECIAL STORY
JUST FOR YOU
with
LOVE
From

Riddle Smiles

Including a funny riddle in your child's lunch bag is a great way to brighten their day. What better riddle to choose than a food related one. Here's a bunch of funny food riddles to choose from. You could include the answer, tell them when they get home or send it the next day.

Why couldn't the orange get up the hill?

It ran out of juice.

What has four wheels and flies?

A garbage truck.

If all the letters in the alphabet were invited to a tea party, which of them would be late?

U,V,W,X,Y,Z. They all come after T.

What drink do frogs like best?

Croak - a -cola

Why did the snail put an "S" on his car?

So everyone would say,
"Look at the S - car - go."

What did the tomato say to his friend?

You go ahead.
I'll ketchup.

Riddle Smiles

What did the hot dog say when he won the race?

I'm the weiner.

Which are the kindest vegetables?

Care-ots

What should a tight rope walker eat?

A balanced diet.

Which hand do you stir your chocolate milk with?

Neither, I use a spoon.

What did the Mommy Olive say to the Baby Olive?

O - Live - you.

How do you mend a Jack-o-lantern?

With a pumpkin patch.

Straw Smiles

Cut out shapes and hole punch them to fit over a colorful straw you include in your child's lunch.

YOU ARE MY STAR

I LOVE YOU

Super Math Whiz

I'LL ALWAYS HAVE TIME FOR YOU.

Everyway I look at it, you are very special to me.

Super Star Smiles

A perfect five point star in five easy steps. Add a starstruck message for your child and put it in their lunch.

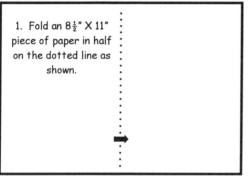

1. Fold an 8½" X 11" piece of paper in half on the dotted line as shown.

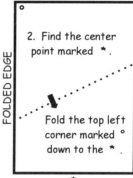

2. Find the center point marked * .

FOLDED EDGE

Fold the top left corner marked ° down to the * .

3. Fold the triangle marked ✗ on the dotted line.

4. Fold the piece marked ▯ on the dotted line.

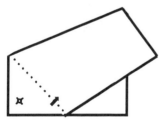

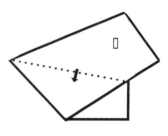

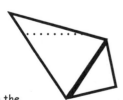

5. Cut on the dotted line.

Special Occasion Smiles

Many things in life revolve around holidays and special occasions. Activities at school are often tied into holidays and Teachers sometimes plan their lessons around holiday themes. Use the following idea to highlight holidays or other special occasions.

Heart Strings

Using the full size patterns given here, cut out 2 copies of each of the 4 hearts. Lay a string along the back of one set of the hearts and tape or glue it to each heart. Leave an 8 cm (3") length of string between each of the hearts. Glue the second set of hearts to the back of their matching one, putting glue only along the bottom edges so they form an envelope for the smaller hearts to fit into.

You could use this idea to cut out other shapes such as pumpkins, bells, snowmen, crosses, eggs, trees, stars, wreaths, fruit, gingerbread houses or men, cornucopia or turkeys. Use your imagination to come up with your own designs. Children would have fun making them for friends.

Choosing a Lunch Container

When choosing a lunch bag and containers, ask yourself the following questions.

1. Are they sturdy enough to stand up to daily use?
2. Are they well designed?
3. Will they be easy to clean?
4. Will it keep the food fresh?
5. Does it meet the needs of the person who will use it?
6. Is it roomy enough to hold everything?
7. Is it easy to open and close?
8. Are they leak proof?

Pack an Earth Friendly Lunch

One of the best ways to have a positive effect on the environment is to teach your children how to be a wise consumer. One way to do this is to pack an earth friendly lunch, whenever possible.

Things to Avoid

- ☒ Plastic Wrap
- ☒ Plastic Bags
- ☒ Aluminum Foil
- ☒ Wax Paper
- ☒ Disposable Cutlery
- ☒ Individually Packaged Items
- ☒ Tetra Pack Juices
- ☒ Paper Bags
- ☒ Paper Napkins

Things to Use

- ☑ Reuseable Lunch Bag
- ☑ Reuseable Containers
- ☑ Reuseable Cutlery
- ☑ Cloth Napkins
- ☑ Thermos

Lunch Bag Pattern

Making your own lunch bag can be lots of fun. They are so easy, you could have a different one for each day of the week. Use a medium weight fabric, possibly a waterproof one. For a special treat, make shaped bags for holidays such as a heart shaped one for Valentines or a Christmas stocking. Use the following pattern to make a lined lunch bag with a fold down flap that closes with velcro.

Materials Needed

2 pieces of fabric 64 cm X 30 cm (25" X 12") each
> One piece will be used for the outer bag and the other will be for the lining.

1 piece of fabric 20 cm X 18 cm (8" X 7")
> This piece will be sewn to form the flap.

Velcro 15 cm (6") long for closure

Overview of Directions: All seam allowances are 1.25 cm ($\frac{1}{2}$"). The velcro is attached to the outer bag and flap before the bags are sewn. The outer bag and lining are sewn separately. The flap is sewn and attached to the outer bag. The outer bag and lining are sewn together.

Lunch Bag with fold down flap and velcro closure.

Lunch Bag Pattern (cont'd)

1. Cut the fabric pieces to the measurements shown in the materials list.

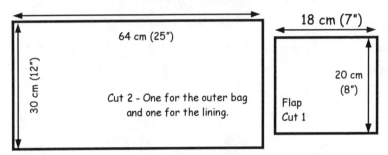

2. Make a copy of the Lunch Bag Template and place it on the outer bag and lining fabric as shown here. Cut away the four black triangles from both pieces of fabric. The template will need to be moved four times on each piece of fabric. Mark the fabric at the (✷) on the template.

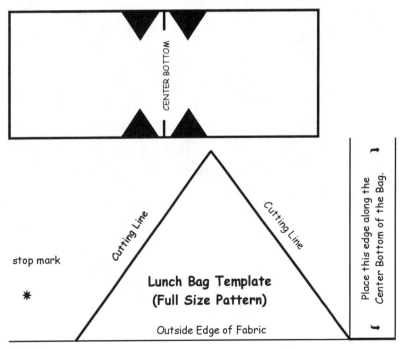

68

Lunch Bag Pattern (cont'd)

3. Center the soft loop piece of the velcro on the right side of the outer fabric piece as shown below and stitch in place. The bottom edge of the velcro is sewn 6.25 cm (2½") below the top edge of the bag.

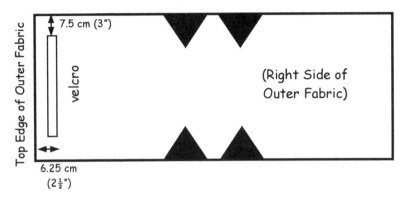

4. Stitch the hook piece of velcro to the right side of the inner flap as shown below. The bottom edge of the velcro should be sewn 6 cm (2½") from the bottom edge of the flap.

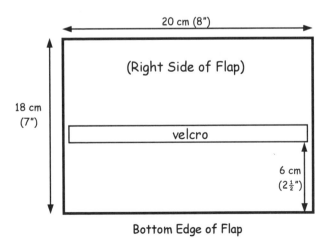

Lunch Bag Pattern (cont'd)

5. Working with the fabric piece for the outside of the bag only, fold the right sides together along the center bottom. Stitch both side seams along the arrow lines as shown below. The (✱) on the template is the stop point for stitching. It is 1.25 cm (½") away from the bottom point of the triangle cutout and the seam allowance.

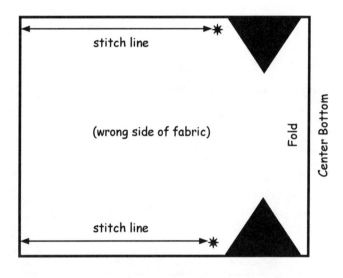

6. Following the diagrams on the next page, refold the bag along the Lines Marked "A" bringing the two sides of each of the cutout triangle shapes together. Using the bottom diagram as a guide, stitch along each of the four arrow lines as shown. Each line should be stitched separately from Line A to the (✱). The side seam should be folded back away from the stitching.

Lunch Bag Pattern (cont'd)

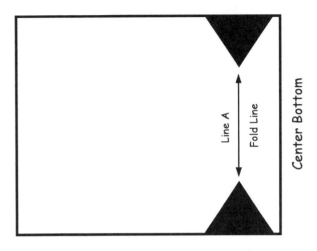

Side View of Bag

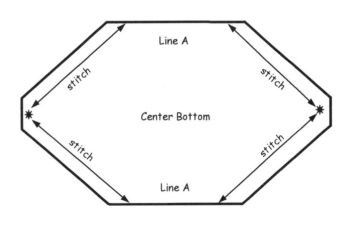

Bottom View of Bag

7. Repeat Steps 5 and 6 to stitch the bag lining.

Lunch Bag Pattern (cont'd)

8. To stitch the flap, fold it in half with right sides together and stitch the sides closed on the lines shown in the diagram below. Turn the flap right sides out. Top stitch along the sides and folded edge. To attach the flap to the outer bag, center the top edges of the flap on the right side of the back of the top edge of the bag. The velcro should be facing out.

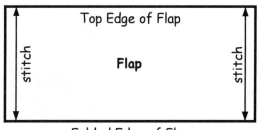

9. Turn the lining bag right side out and place it inside the outer bag, with the right sides facing each other. Stitch the two bags together along the top sides and front. Start and stop the stitching at the edges of the flap but do not stitch across the flap.

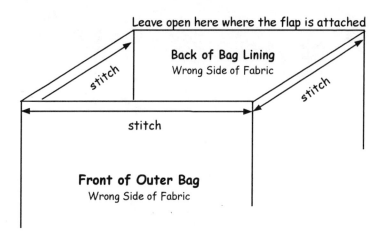

Lunch Bag Pattern (cont'd)

10. Pull both the inner and outer bags through the opening to turn them right sides out. Fold the seam allowance for the bag and flap into the opening and top stitch around the top of the bag to close the opening and give the bag a finished look. If desired, you can topstitch down each corner of the bag and across the side bottoms. Now, you have your very own washable, reuseable lunch bag. They make great gifts, too. Use them as the gift bag and pack them full of lots of surprises. Happy Baggin' It.

If you like to sew and want to get really creative, you might add:

- a handle made from webbing.

- a plastic pocket to hold a picture.

- a zipper pocket to hold milk money, novelty treats or notes.

Disposable Lunches
For field trips or other times when disposable lunches are required, use stickers, rubber stamps and markers to decorate a paper sack.

Cloth Napkins

Eating lunch can be messy so including a colorful napkin is a practical way to brighten up a dull lunch.

Choose a colorful, absorbent fabric. Cut out a 25 cm (10") square. Use the serger to finish the edges. If you don't have a serger, cut out the napkin with pinking shears or sew a narrow hem. Make a variety so you have one for each day of the week. To save packaging material, wrap dry crackers and cookies in the napkins.

For a special treat, put a surprise inside a cardboard tube. Roll the napkin around the tube and tie the ends with licorice shoelaces.

SURPRISE INSIDE

Family Photo
Children, who are away all day for the first time, will appreciate a family photo inserted in a plastic sleeve and taped to the inside of their lunch container.

Pop Top Magnet
If your child has a metal desk, attach a magnet to the back of a Juice Can lid; the kind that pops off when you pull the plastic strip. Glue a picture on the front or write something fun on it.

Making Food Fun

Kids are more likely to eat food when it looks interesting and tasty. The food in packed lunches doesn't have to look boring. Here are some ways to make food look fun to eat. These ideas are great for packed lunches, school snack days and after school snacks.

Sandwich Surprise

Use cookie cutters to cut interesting designs and shapes in sandwiches, or cut the sandwiches into interesting shapes.

Alphabet Snacks

Cook bread dough, pretzels, biscuits or pancakes in the shape of your child's initials. For school snacks, make one for each child in the class.

Cupcake Surprise

Wrap a message in waxpaper and insert it into a cupcake by making a slit in the top before icing it. So your child doesn't eat the paper, put a note on the outside telling them there's a surprise inside.

Cone Cakes

Bake cake batter in flat bottomed ice cream cones. Set them in muffin tins and fill 2/3 full with batter. Bake at 350° F for 20 minutes or until done. Ice if desired and top with sprinkles or a cherry.

Orange Buddies

Glue paper shapes to an orange or use a permanent marker to decorate it with a pumpkin or smiley face.

Bunny Eggs

For Easter, glue bunny ears and feet on a plastic egg. Use a permanent marker to draw a face. Put special treats inside the egg.

Jack O' Sandwiches

For Halloween, cut out a pumpkin face from one slice of bread. Sandwich cheese between the slices.

Surprise Boo

Wrap food or a treat in a white napkin and tie it with an orange ribbon. Draw a face on the napkin.

Cookie Countdown

To count down the days until Christmas, use icing to pipe the numbers from 1 - 24 on to cookies. Send a cookie in your child's lunch with the number for the days left until Christmas.

Heart Cakes

For Valentines, cook cupcakes in a heart shape by inserting a small ball of foil or a marble down the edge between the paper cup and the baking tins. Fill half full with batter. When the batter rises, it will keep the heart shape.

Tin Can Heart

Make a heart shaped cookie cutter by removing both ends from a tin can and bending it into a heart shape. Use to cut out shapes from red gelatin or cookie dough.

Banana Dogs

Spread peanut butter and honey on
a hot dog bun. Send a banana along
in the lunch. Your child can peel
the banana and put it on the bun.

Biscuit Bunnies and Bears

Cut biscuits into circles. Cut the
circles and piece together as shown
to make a biscuit bear or bunny. Use
raisins, currants, and slivered almonds
to decorate before baking.

Bunny

Use one circle for the head and cut one
circle in half and shape it to make the
ears. Decorate and bake.

Bear

Use two circles for the head and body.
Cut one circle into quarters and use for
the arms and legs. Cut another circle into
quarters and use two of the pieces to
make the ears. Decorate and bake.

Bread Stick Roll Ups

Roll sliced meat and cheese
around the outside of a
bread stick. Secure with a
ribbon cut from a green
onion. With older children,
you could secure them with
toothpicks.

Dog Wrap

Roll out pizza or bread dough in a long rope and wrap it around a weiner. Put a slice of cheese along the top of the wrapped weiner and bake until the dough is cooked.

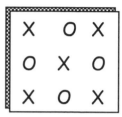

Pizza Tic Tac Toe

Make pizza dough into a square shape. Put on the Sauce and Cheese. Top with Green Pepper Strips for the X's and Pepperoni Slices for the O's.

Marshmallow Hedgehogs

Spread peanut butter on a large marshamallow and roll it in plain or toasted coconut or puffed rice cereal.

Fruity Salad Drink

Make fruit salad from any combination of fruit. Cover it with fruit juice. Serve in a cup with a spoon. The fruit stays fresh and it's a drink and snack in one.

Stuffed Apples

Cut the top off an apple just as you would when carving a pumpkin. Use a melon baller or sharp knife to hollow out the core. Fill the hollow with peanut butter, raisins or cream cheese. Or make an **Inside-Out Caramel Apple** by filling the inside with melted caramels.

Pancake Roll Ups

When I was young, I liked to go with my dad when he hauled grain to town. Often he would be ready to leave before I had my breakfast so mom would quickly spread a pancake with butter and jelly and roll it up for me to eat on the road. I still like to eat cold pancakes with jelly. Maybe your kids would too. My friend, Brenda, who is a teacher, served small pancakes with apple sauce, cinnamon and whipped cream for her son's ECS snack and it was a big hit.

Bagel Buddies

Slice bagels in half. Spread with your favorite topping and decorate to look like faces. Use Carrot Curls for the hair. Chunks of vegetables can be used for the features. Olive slices work well for the eyes and red pepper slices for the lips. Use your imagination or supply the fixings and let the children make their own.

Millenium Bugs

Use vegetables to create edible millenium bugs. To make a caterpillar, spread celery with peanut butter or cheese and decorate with raisins for eyes and dry chow mein noodles for antennae. Use seeds or small chunks of carrot for the stripes. Make your caterpillar furry by sticking grated carrot onto it. To make a ladybug, cut a cherry tomato in half. Push sunflower seeds into it for spots and add chow mein noodle antennae. The possibilities are only limited by your imaginations.

Edible Necklaces

String dougnut shaped dry cereal on licorice laces and tie in a knot.

Hard Boiled Mice

Cut a hard boiled egg in half and place it cut side down on a bed of lettuce or sprouts. Decorate with ham circles for ears and a ham triangle for the nose. Cut small slits in the eggs to hold the features in place. Use strips of chives for whiskers and sunflower seeds for the eyes. Use a cheese string or ham strip for the tail.

Cupcake Softballs

Ice cupcakes with white icing. Flatten licorice shoestrings with a rolling pin and snip the edges to look like lacing. Place the lacing on the icing so it looks like stitching.

Pinwheels

Slice bread the long way of the loaf. Slightly flatten slices with a rolling pin. Spread with filling and roll up. Wrap and chill overnight or freeze. To serve, cut the rolls into $\frac{1}{2}$" slices.

Celery Car

Spread celery with cheese or peanut butter and sprinkle with raisins. Use toothpicks to add carrot circles for wheels. When using toothpicks in food, caution children to be careful and supervise.

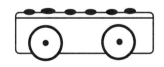

Hot Snacks

Many schools are equipped with microwaves and conventional ovens, making it possible to serve hot snacks. Here are some ideas that are sure to please.

- Small bowls of Soup with Fish Shaped Crackers.
- Chili, Stew
- Mini Pizzas
- French Toast with Butter and Jelly or sprinkled with Icing Sugar. To make French Toast, crack an Egg on a plate. Stir in 1 T. Milk. Coat both sides of Bread. Toast on a hot, lightly greased griddle. Turn until golden brown on both sides.
- Cinnamon Toast. Mix 3 T. Sugar and 1 tsp. Cinnamon in a shaker. Butter the toast and shake on the Sugar and Cinnamon mixture.
- Hot Chocolate
- Place Taco Chips on a plate. Sprinkle with Grated Cheese and melt in the microwave. Add Chopped Onion, Tomato, Shredded Lettuce and Taco Sauce or Salsa.
- Toast Bread. Put a Cheese Slice on top or spread with Cheese Spread. Broil until lightly brown and bubbly. Top with a thin slice of Tomato and a sprinkle of Parmesan.
- Chicken Wings, Drumsticks and Ribs
- Hot Cereals such as Oatmeal or Cream of Wheat

MAKE IT YOURSELF RECIPES

I CAN COOK PRETTY MUCH ANYTHING IF THE MAIN INGREDIENTS ARE PEANUT BUTTER AND JELLY.

Special Concerns

This book does not address special dietary problems related to food allergy, intolerance or diseases. If you have any concerns about your child's special dietary requirements or nutritional needs, consult your doctor or a professional registered dietitian.

When I am cooking and baking, I keep nutrition in mind. I like to experiment with recipes to make them more nutritious by reducing the amounts of fat, sugar and salt and by adding or substituting healthier ingredients.

When it comes to making decisions in life, I like the principle of moderation in all things. (Phil. 4:5) My grandpa was a great role model for moderation and lived a healthy life, retiring from farming in his eighties and passing away at 90. Whenever a huge meal with lots of tempting goodies was served, Grandpa always took a moderate serving and never over stuffed himself.

I also appreciated my father-in-law's attitude. Clinton was one of triplet boys born in 1906 to a family that already had brother/sister twins and a sister. He lived an active, healthy life and raised 10 children with his wife, Dorothy. Clinton passed away in his 86th year. Despite adult diabetes, he would occasionally indulge himself with a second helping of dessert. Being reminded of his health by a fellow diner would prompt him to say, "Oh well, you only live 'til you die."

Both Grandpa and Clinton were men of faith who took a practical approach to living. Healthy eating is important for lifelong health but like anything else it can be overemphasized, taking the pleasure away from an enjoyable, social activity. Keep informed, use commonsense, eat healthy, be active and encourage your children to do the same.

Professional Nutrition Advice
Alison Craig, B.Sc., R.D.

Healthy eating provides our children with the energy and nutrients they need to grow, be active and feel good about themselves. School lunches can be an important part of a child's daily food intake, giving their bodies the fuel needed to stay alert and receptive to learning. Choosing nutritious and appealing items to pack in our children's lunches is a challenging, daily routine.

A nutritious lunch should aim to provide choices from each of the four basic food groups: **Vegetables and Fruits, Grain Products, Milk Products** and **Meat and Alternatives**. It is recommended that more of our food energy should come from complex carbohydrates which means emphasizing more servings of Grain Products, Vegetables and Fruit. The amount of food and the number of servings children need will depend on their body size, gender, how fast they are growing and how physically active they are. Items such as soft drinks, jam, candies, butter, oil, margarine, high fat or high salt snack foods such as potato chips, and condiments such as ketchup are referred to as **Other Foods**. These foods can be part of a healthy eating pattern as long as they are used to complement a nutritious diet, rather than replace choices from the four main food groups.

One of the keys to good nutrition is variety. Choosing a variety of foods from each of the food groups will supply all the nutrients growing bodies need. Each food has something different to offer in terms of nutrients. To provide variety, serve foods with different tastes, textures and colors. Expose your children to new tastes by introducing new foods along with familiar foods.

With over 15,000 food products to choose from at the supermarket, it is easier to put variety into our diets but more challenging to become familiar with all the choices available and how they rate nutritionally. Ingredients are required to be listed on labels in descending order of amount. Checking the first three ingredients will give you a fairly good idea of what's inside. Knowing the ingredients will help you decide if a particular food should be a regular part of your overall diet or a complement to it.

Contact local health departments for publications that will give you further assistance in reading labels and planning nutritious meals. Taking a nutrition tour, offered by some grocery stores and guided by a registered dietitian, is an excellent way to find out what is available and where it can fit into your diet. If there is concern that a child is not getting the nutrients needed to grow and be healthy, a registered dietitian can assess your child's food intake and give recommendations to help meet the child's nutritional needs.

Childhood is the best time to learn healthy eating habits. At an early age, children are learning in the classroom about what healthy living means and how to make nutritious food choices. Setting a positive example at home will reinforce what they are learning at school and help them develop positive, lifelong eating habits. There are many other factors that influence what children will eat. These include taste, social influences, media messages and of course, their peers. When school children eat lunch together, it is a social activity and one to be enjoyed.

Alison Craig, B.Sc., R.D. lives in Edmonton, with her husband and four active children. She is a nutrition consultant and also conducts grocery store nutrition tours for adults and school groups. In addition to her private practice, Alison has had several years of experience as a clinical dietitian in a hospital setting.

Metric/Imperial Measurement

These are the acceptable, but not exact, metric substitutions in case you only cook in metric. Some recipes convert favorably, while others do not. I'm the kind of cook who likes to throw everything in a bowl at once and my measurement motto is "close enough". Food disappears so quickly at our house that, after the initial disappointment, we hardly notice the recipes that don't quite work out.

Approximate Measurement Conversions

1 Cup	250 ml
½ Cup	125 ml
⅓ Cup	75 ml
¼ Cup	50 ml

1 tsp.	5 ml
½ tsp.	2 ml
¼ tsp.	1 ml
1 T.	15 ml

- Cup is the standard 8 fl. oz.
- Teaspoon is abbreviated as tsp.
- Tablespoon is abbreviated as T.

Approximate Weight Conversions

¼ LB.	100 grams
½ LB.	250 grams
1 LB.	500 grams
2 LB.	1 Kilogram

Approximate Temperature Conversions

Fahrenheit	Celsius	Fahrenheit	Celsius
200	100	375	190
275	140	400	200
300	150	425	220
325	160	450	230
350	180		

 ## Safe Storage Temperatures

To keep food fresh as long as possible use the following guidelines for appliance temperatures.

Refrigerator Temperature: 40° Fahrenheit, 4° Celsius
Freezer Temperature: 0° Fahrenheit, -18° Celsius

To avoid dangerous bacteria growth, keep food colder than 40° Fahrenheit (4° Celsius) and hotter than 140° Fahrenheit (60° Celsius).

Beverages

A quality thermos is a worthwhile investment. Buying drinks in bulk and pouring them into a thermos is an inexpensive way to provide a hot or cold drink for lunch. For cold drinks, pre-chill the thermos by filling it with ice water and letting it stand for several minutes. Pour out the ice water and pour in the cold drink. To pre-heat the thermos, fill it with very hot water and let stand for a few minutes.

To make crushed ice, fill a clean milk carton half full of water and freeze it. When frozen, drop it on a cement floor several times. Refreshing when added to a cold drink on a hot summer day.

Plastic Pop Top Bottles are great containers for eliminating spills on a night stand or while travelling. For trips on hot summer days, we fill them halfway and freeze. Allowing only water in the car has saved a lot of sticky cleanups.

Refreshing Lunchtime Drinks

- Cold Water
- Milk
- Iced Tea
- Hot Apple Juice packed with a Cinnamon Stick

- Lemonade
- Chocolate Milk
- Hot Chocolate
- Fruit Juice and Seltzer

Spicy Fruit Blend

1 Cup	Milk
1	Banana
1 tsp.	Honey (or 1-2 tsp. Sugar)
Dash	Cinnamon
¼ tsp.	Vanilla

Puree above ingredients in a blender or food processor.
Pour into a pre-chilled thermos.
Variation: Substitute Ice Cream for the Yogurt.
Substitute Orange for the Milk.

Cocoa Syrup

½ Cup	Cocoa
1 Cup	Corn Syrup
½ Cup	Boiling Water
½ tsp.	Salt
½ tsp.	Vanilla

Mix the Cocoa and Corn Syrup in the top of a double boiler.
Add the Boiling Water to the Syrup mixture. Cook in the
double boiler for 10 minutes. Remove from heat and add the
Salt and Vanilla. Store in fridge.
Hot Cocoa: Add 1 T. of Cocoa Syrup to 1 Cup Hot Milk.

Yogurt Shake

$\frac{1}{2}$ Cup	Milk
$\frac{1}{2}$ Cup	Yogurt
$\frac{1}{2}$	Banana
$\frac{1}{2}$ Cup	Strawberries or Blueberries

Puree above ingredients in a blender or food processor. Pour into a pre-chilled thermos.

Variation: Add $\frac{1}{2}$ Cup Ice Cream or substitute Ice Cream for the Yogurt.

Orange Fluff

2 Cups	Milk
2 T.	Honey
1 Cup	Ice Cream
$\frac{1}{4}$ Cup	Frozen Orange Juice Concentrate

Combine well in a blender or food processor and pour into a pre-chilled thermos.

Pineapple Citrus Tea

This punch is great for parties. Children feel special when treated to a punch served in a beautiful punch bowl.

3	Tea Bags
6 Cups	Boiling Water
1 Cup	White Sugar
6 Cups	Orange Juice, Unsweetened
6 Cups	Pineapple Juice, Unsweetened
3 Cups	Lemon Juice, Unsweetened
2	Bottles Gingerale (2 L Size)

Combine the Boiling Water and Tea Bags and steep for five minutes. Remove the Tea Bags and add the Sugar. Cool. Add the Orange, Pineapple and Lemon Juices. Put in a large Punch Bowl and add the Gingerale just before serving.

Variation: Substitute other favorite juices for the ones listed above.

Colorful Cubes

To make colorful ice cubes, put Maraschino Cherries, Grapes or Strawberries in ice cube trays and fill with Orange Juice. Freeze. You can also put a Maraschino Cherry in the center of a Pineapple Ring placed in a muffin tin. Top up with Juice and freeze. Another way to make a colorful ice cube is to freeze layers of different colored juices in the bottom of a plastic pail. Let one layer freeze before adding the next color juice.

Breads

Sandwiches form the basis for many bag lunches. There are so many flavors and styles of bread available that sandwiches never need to be boring. I love to bake my own breads and with quick rising yeasts, it's easier and less time consuming than ever. It's fun to experiment with the variety of grains and flours available. I often substitute some of these specialty flours for part of the flour in recipes. Many people are using Bread Machines to serve up fresh, delicious bread everyday. They provide convenience for making single loaves. I prefer to make bread the old fashioned way because the batches are larger and I can always have some handy in the freezer for last minute company or school lunches.

Cinnamon Twists

Use the Pizza Dough recipe on the next page to make these delicious golden twists which taste great served hot or packed cold in a lunch.

Greased Baking Sheet, Bake at 350° for 15 Minutes

Pizza or Bun Dough

$\frac{1}{4}$ Cup   Butter, Melted

$\frac{1}{2}$ Cup   Brown Sugar

4 tsp.   Cinnamon

Roll out dough to $\frac{1}{4}$" thickness and 12" X 16" in size. Brush with the Melted Butter. Combine Brown Sugar and Cinnamon and sprinkle evenly over the Butter. Rest the dough for 6 Minutes. Cut lengthwise into 3 strips that measure 16" X 4". Cut each of these strips into 16 strips that measure 4" X 1". Twist each strip one full turn and place on a greased baking sheet. Cover and rise until doubled.

Pizza Bread Dough

This dough is so versatile. I use it for Pizza Crust, Cheese Bread, Cinnamon Twists and Pretzels. This batch makes enough for 4 Medium Pizzas. I usually make 2 pizzas and use the leftover for bread sticks or pretzels. I sometimes shape pieces of dough into mini pizza crusts and freeze them on a cookie tray. When frozen, I bag them until needed. For a snack, thaw, add toppings and bake in the toaster oven. Cooked mini pizzas may also be frozen and sent in lunches.

Breads

Greased Pizza Pan/Baking Sheet, Bake at 475° for 6-10 Minutes	

2 Cups	Water (warm)
5 Cups	Flour
2 T.	Quick Rising Yeast
1 T.	Oil
1 T.	Sugar
1½ tsp.	Salt
1	Egg

Mix Flour, Yeast, Oil, Sugar, Salt and Egg. Add Warm Water and mix until smooth and elastic. Rise in a warm place until double; about 20-30 minutes. Punch down and rest 10 minutes. With oiled hands, shape pieces of dough in flat circles for pizza or long round strips for bread sticks. Place on a well greased baking sheet. Top with pizza sauce, grated cheese and any toppings you wish to add; mushrooms, green pepper, onion, pepperoni, ham, pineapple. For breadsticks, top with grated cheese or sprinkle with garlic salt. You can make pretzels by rolling pieces of dough into long snakes and twisting into pretzel shapes. Brush with Egg White and sprinkle with coarse salt.

Pizza Sauce

My youngest child likes pizza sauce and grated cheese melted on bread in the microwave. To make individual servings of pizza sauce, I freeze it in small blobs on a cookie sheet and bag after it is frozen. The blobs thaw quickly and you only have to thaw the amount you need. This works well with store bought sauces or homemade.

Stove Top Required. Yield: 1½-2 Cups	

2 T.	Butter or Oil
2½ lbs.	Fresh Tomatoes, chopped
½ Cup	Onion, finely diced
1 Clove	Garlic, minced
¼ Cup	Tomato Paste
1 Small	Grated Carrot
1	Bay Leaf
1 tsp.	Basil
½ tsp.	Oregano
¼ tsp.	Each Salt & Pepper, or to taste
1 tsp.	Sugar
Dash	Hot Pepper Sauce

Sauté Tomatoes, Onion and Garlic in Butter, until tender. Add the remaining ingredients and simmer for 35-45 Minutes. This sauce should be used the same day or frozen for later use.

Pita Bread

Pita Pockets are fun to make and kids are always surprised to see the bread puff up and cook to form a pocket. They are a nice change from bread or buns.

Breads

Ungreased Baking Sheet, Bake at 450° for 3 Min. per side

$3\frac{1}{4}$-$3\frac{3}{4}$ Cups	Flour
1 T.	Quick Rising Yeast
$1\frac{1}{4}$ Cups	Warm Water
$\frac{1}{4}$ Cup	Shortening
1 tsp.	Salt
1 T.	Sugar

Combine ingredients, adding enough flour to make a soft dough. Knead 3-5 Minutes until dough is smooth and elastic. Cover and rest for 15 Minutes. Divide the dough into 12 equal size balls. Cover the balls with a damp cloth and rest for 10 Minutes. Gently flatten the balls, being careful not to crease the dough. Cover and rest 10 Minutes. Remove 2 flattened balls from under the cloth and roll them from the center to the edges to a 7" diameter. Place circles on a cookie sheet and bake 3 Minutes. Turn and bake 3 more minutes or until puffy and golden brown. Store in fridge or freezer.

Off the Wall Pizza

For a crazy but good pizza, bake a pizza dough crust. Spread it with peanut butter. Add Banana Circles and drizzle with warm Honey. Add Raisins, Sunflower Seeds, Coconut, Nuts or Cheese if desired. Enjoy.

Braided Bread

This dough is easy to handle and cooks into a soft delicious bread. This recipe came from my sister-in-law, Norma. I taught at a school near George and Norma's farm and spent many weekends as a guest at their house. Norma is a terrific cook and she taught me a lot about cooking and being a good hostess. Their "the coffeepot is always on" reputation means baking never lasts more than a day. It was an ideal place to practice my skills and try new recipes.

Greased Baking Sheet, Bake at 350° for 25-30 Minutes

3 Cups	Warm Milk
1 Cup	Warm Water
½ Cup	Sugar
4 tsp.	Salt
½ Cup	Butter
4	Eggs
2 T.	Quick Rising Yeast
8-10 Cups	Flour

Mix above ingredients, adding enough flour to make a soft dough. Place in a lightly greased bowl to rise until doubled. Punch down and divide into 4 equal pieces. Cover and let rest for 10 minutes. Divide each of the pieces into 3 equal pieces and form into long rope shapes. Braid the dough ropes. Tuck ends under and place on a greased baking sheet. Repeat with remaining pieces of dough. Rise until doubled. Bake.

Variation: Brush loaves with Egg Yolk beaten with 2 T. Water and sprinkle with Sesame or Poppy seeds. You can also substitute 3 Cups Oatmeal for some of the flour.

Snowflake Buns

This recipe is adapted from one my sister-in-law, Norma uses. This is a double batch because if you go to the trouble to make buns, you want to be able to enjoy them for a few days. They also freeze well. With this recipe, I make 2 trays of buns and use the rest to make Cinnamon Buns. For Cinnamon Buns, I roll out the remaining dough, spread it with melted Butter and sprinkle with Brown Sugar and Cinnamon. Roll up Jelly Roll style, cut into 1" slices and bake in a greased pan.

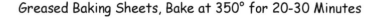

Greased Baking Sheets, Bake at 350° for 20-30 Minutes	

3 Cups	Warm Water
2 Cups	Warm Milk
2 T.	Quick Rising Yeast
13-14 Cups	Flour, Approximately
$\frac{2}{3}$ Cup	Butter
$\frac{2}{3}$ Cup	Sugar
4 tsp.	Salt
4	Eggs

Combine ingredients, adding enough flour to make a soft dough. Knead 3-5 Minutes until dough is smooth and elastic. Cover and rise until doubled. Knead down and rest 10 minutes. Form Buns and Cinnamon Buns if desired. Let rise until doubled. Bake.

White or Whole Wheat Bread

All of the recipes in this book work well with white, whole wheat or multi-grain flours. I often add one of these specialty flours in place of a portion of the white flour. When using whole grain flours, you won't need quite as much flour to make the same stiffness of dough. I like to experiment and write notes in my recipe books so I know what I did last time. Favorite cookbooks and recipes often become cherished family keepsakes and with handwritten notes from the cook they are even more enjoyable.

| 4 - Greased Loaf Pans, Bake at 350° for 25-30 Minutes |

2 Cups	Warm Milk
2 Cups	Warm Water
¼ Cup	Sugar
3 tsp.	Salt
¼ Cup	Butter
1 T.	Quick Rising Yeast
6-7 Cups	Flour

Mix above ingredients, adding enough flour to make a soft dough. Place in a lightly greased bowl to rise until doubled. Punch down and divide into 4 equal pieces. Cover and let rest for 10 minutes. Form pieces of dough into loaves and place in greased loaf pans. Let rise until doubled. Bake.

Tea Biscuits

Biscuits make a nice addition to a meal or they can be used as an alternative to a sandwich in lunches.

Ungreased Baking Sheet, 425° for 12-15 Min.	

2 Cups   Flour

4 tsp.   Baking Powder

1 tsp.   Salt

½ Cup   Butter or Shortening

1 Cup   Milk

Mix Flour, Baking Powder and Salt. Cut in the Butter. Add the Milk and knead for 1 Minute. Roll to ½" thickness and cut with a round cookie cutter. Place on baking sheet and bake until golden. Serve hot from the oven or cold with jam or honey. Send in lunches with a thermos of soup.

Variations: 1. Add ½ Cup Shredded Cheese

2. Add ½ Cup Shredded Cheese, ¼ tsp. Oregano and ¼ tsp. Basil.

3. Add ½ Cup Raisins or Currants.

4. Mix 1 T. Melted Butter, 1 T. Brown Sugar and a shake of Cinnamon. Roll dough to ¼" thickness. Cut out circles. Place a small amount of the cinnamon mixture on the top of each circle. Stack 2 circles on top of each other and bake.

Scones

Scones are great served hot from the oven or cold with butter and jam. A nice addition when packed with a thermos of hot chili or stew.

Greased Baking Sheet, Bake 400° for 12-15 Min., Yield: 16

2 Cups	Flour
$\frac{1}{4}$ Cup	Sugar
1 T.	Baking Powder
$\frac{1}{2}$ tsp.	Salt
$\frac{1}{4}$ Cup	Butter
2	Eggs
$\frac{1}{2}$ Cup	Sour Milk (1 tsp. Vinegar & enough Milk to make $\frac{1}{2}$ Cup.)
$\frac{1}{2}$ Cup	Dried Fruit such as Raisins, Chopped Dates, Currants, Chopped Apples and Cinnamon, Fresh Blueberries, or Shredded Cheese.

Mix Flour, Sugar, Baking Powder and Salt until well blended. Cut in Butter. Add the Eggs and Milk and knead for 1 Minute. Mix in the Fruit or Cheese. Divide the dough in half and roll each half to $\frac{1}{2}$" thickness forming a 7" circle. Place circles on a greased baking sheet and cut into 8 wedge-shaped pieces. Bake until golden brown. I like to divide the dough and mix different ingredients into each piece.
Variation: Use Shredded Cheese, $\frac{1}{4}$ tsp. Oregano and $\frac{1}{4}$ tsp. Basil to make a spicy scone.

Crêpes

Crêpes can be served warm or cold, as a main dish, appetizer or dessert. Almost anything goes with them. They travel well and can be frozen by stacking them between layers of wax paper.

8" Crepe/Frying Pan, Stove Top Required.

---

1 Cup	Flour
$\frac{1}{4}$ tsp.	Salt
3	Eggs, Beaten
1 T.	Melted Butter
$1\frac{1}{2}$ Cups	Milk

Combine Flour and Salt. Whisk in Eggs, Milk and Butter and continue beating until smooth. Place lightly greased Crepe Pan over Medium heat. Pour 2 T. of batter into pan, tilting the pan to spread the batter over the bottom. Cook until the bottom is golden and the top is no longer shiny. Loosen and turn crêpe. Cook until golden. Remove from pan. Continue until all the crêpes are cooked. To serve, roll crepes around vegetables, meat fillings, or cream cheese, sour cream and herbs.

Variation: To make dessert crêpes, add 1 tsp. Sugar and $\frac{1}{2}$ tsp. Vanilla to the Batter. Serve with Applesauce, Fresh Fruit, Pie Filling, Puddings or Jam. Add Maple Syrup and Whipped Cream for a special treat.

Waffles/Pancakes

One of our favorite, 'make it in a hurry', meals is waffles, fresh fruit and whipped cream served with bacon and eggs. Go heavy on the fruit, and light on the whipped cream and bacon, so the calories don't add up too quickly.

Waffle Maker or Grill Required

1½ Cups	Flour	
2 T.	Sugar	
3 tsp.	Baking Powder	
½ tsp.	Salt	
2	Eggs, Beaten	
¼ Cup	Oil	
1½ Cups	Milk (enough to make 2 Cups of liquid when added to the Eggs and Oil)	

Combine Flour, Sugar, Baking Powder and Salt. Whisk in the Egg, Oil and Milk mixture and beat until smooth. Cook on a pre-heated griddle. Cook waffles until steaming stops. Turn pancakes when they are puffed and full of bubbles. Serve warm with fresh Fruit, Applesauce, Syrup and Whipped Cream. Serve cold by spreading with Jam and rolling up.

Pancake Variations: Add Blueberries, Shredded Cheese, or Chocolate Chips to the batter before cooking.

Cornbread

Cornbread is quick to make and tasty, served warm or cold. It travels well and can be sent in lunches with a thermos of soup.

Muffin Pan, Bake 400° for 15-20 Min.
9" Square Greased Pan, Bake 375° for 25-30 Min.

¾	Cup	Cornmeal
1¼	Cups	Milk
1	Cup	Flour
⅓	Cup	Sugar
1	T.	Baking Powder
½	tsp.	Salt
¼	Cup	Oil
1		Egg

Combine Milk and Cornmeal and let stand for 10 Minutes. Combine Flour, Sugar, Baking Powder and Salt. Stir all ingredients together, until combined. Bake in a square, greased pan or in muffin tins.

Hot Foods

A good quality thermos makes it easy and economical to have a hot lunch. There are a wide variety of foods that can be heated and packed in a thermos to provide a satisfying, change of pace lunch. Many schools provide microwaves for reheating lunch food. However, the amount of time required to reheat many foods can result in significant waiting times. When children are hungry, they often become frustrated. If there are always lineups for the microwave, I think it's better to provide a hot thermos and avoid waiting.

Terrific Hot Food Ideas

Stew	Macaroni	Casseroles
Spaghetti	Scalloped Potatoes	Quiche
Lasagna	Creamed Vegetables	Cooked Meats
Hot Dogs	Stewed Tomatoes	Tacos
Baked Beans	Rice	Pizza
Meatballs	Chicken Parts	Leftovers

- Freeze leftovers in individual portions. You'll have a wide variety of foods available and can easily thaw only the amount you need.
- Prepare a double batch when making a hot meal. Eat one and freeze one for later use. You'll spend less time preparing and cleaning up.
- Pre-heat thermoses with boiling water.
- Pack a hot dog in a thermos of hot water.

Chicken Soup Stock

Making your own soup stock is really quite easy. By making a large batch, you can freeze the stock in soup sized portions ready for later use.

Stove Top Required, Large Soup Pot

Hot Foods

3 LB.	Chicken Carcass (1.5 kg)
8 Cups	Water
2 Stalks	Celery, Chopped
2 Large	Carrots, Chopped
1 Med.	Onion, Chopped Coarse
1 Clove	Garlic
2	Bay Leaves
1 tsp.	Thyme
1 tsp.	Whole Peppercorns

Put all ingredients in a large sauce pan. Bring to a boil. Reduce heat and simmer for 2-3 hours. Strain. Cool and remove fat from the surface. Freeze in desired portions.

Chicken Noodle Soup

There's nothing like a hot thermos of soup on a cold day. Use your own chicken stock or purchased stock to make this delicious soup.

Stove Top Required, Large Soup Pot, Yields 4-6 Servings		

5 Cups	Chicken Soup Stock
1 Large	Onion, Chopped
1 Cup	Diced Carrots
1 Cup	Diced Celery
1 Cup	Boneless Cooked Chicken, Chopped
3	Green Onions, Chopped
1 Cup	Egg Noodles
	Salt and Pepper to taste

Put all ingredients except Noodles in a large pan and bring to a boil. Reduce heat and simmer until vegetables are tender. Add Green Onion and Egg Noodles and cook until noodles are tender. Add Salt and Pepper to taste.

Hot Foods

Beef Soup Stock

So now you've tried the chicken, how about making Beef Stock. Low in additives and high in taste and nutrition.

Stove Top Required, Large Soup Pot

4 LB.	Beef Soup Bones
12 Cups	Water
3 Stalks	Celery, Chopped ($\frac{1}{2}$ tsp. Celery Salt)
3 Large	Carrots, Chopped
1 Large	Onion, Chopped Coarse
1 tsp.	Whole Peppercorns
1 tsp.	Parsley
1 tsp.	Thyme
2 Cloves	Garlic
2	Bay Leaves
2	Whole Cloves

Put all ingredients in a large sauce pan. Bring to a boil. Reduce heat and simmer for 3-4 hours. Froth can be skimmed from the top during cooking if desired. Strain and Cool. Skim fat from the top and discard. Freeze in desired portions.

Hint: Roasting the bones for 1 hour in a 400° oven will add a rich color and flavor to the soup stock.

Beefy Vegetable Soup

A thick beefy soup stuffed full of vegetables provides a rich, nutritious meal on a cold day. Our family loves soup and eats it all year round.

Stove Top Required, Large Soup Pot, Yields 4-6 Servings	

5 Cups	Beef Soup Stock
1 Med.	Onion, Chopped
1 Cup	Carrot, Chopped
$\frac{1}{2}$ Cup	Celery, Chopped
$\frac{1}{2}$ Cup	Vegetable of Choice such as Corn, Turnip, Peas, Beans.
2 Large	Tomatoes, Diced
$\frac{1}{2}$ tsp.	Marjoram
$\frac{1}{2}$ tsp.	Thyme
1 Cup	Pre-Cooked Beef, Chopped Coarse
	Salt & Pepper to Taste

Put all ingredients in a large pot and bring to a boil. Reduce heat and simmer until vegetables are tender. Add Salt and Pepper to taste.

Variation: Add $\frac{1}{2}$ Cup of Pearl Barley with the Vegetables.

Vegetable Soup Stock

This stock is full of vitamins and flavor.

	Stove Top Required, Large Soup Pot	

12	Cups	Water
3	Stalks	Celery, Chopped ($\frac{1}{2}$ tsp. Celery Salt)
4	Large	Carrots, Chopped
1		Apple, Peel and Dice
1	Large	Onion
10		Peppercorns
1	T.	Parsley
2		Bay Leaf

Put all ingredients in a large sauce pan. Bring to a boil. Reduce heat and simmer for 1 hour. Strain and Cool. Freeze in desired portions.

Broccoli Soup

Creamy with lots of Broccoli flavor. If your family loves broccoli, they'll love this soup.

Stove Top Required, Large Soup Pot, Yields 4-6 Servings	

2 T.	Butter
2 T.	Flour
3 Cups	Milk
2 Large	Stocks Broccoli
¼ tsp.	Nutmeg
	Salt & Pepper to taste
1-2 Cups	Vegetable Stock

Sauté Butter and Flour in Sauce Pan until combined. Slowly add Milk, stirring to avoid lumps. Add Broccoli and boil 5 Minutes or until Broccoli is tender. Add Nutmeg. Cool slightly. Pureé in a Blender or Food Processor. Return the Pureé to the Pot and add enough Vegetable Stock to obtain desired consistency.

Wonderful Wonton Soup

This is a favorite. Get your children to help wrap the wontons. They'll enjoy eating it more if they've helped make it.

Stove Top Required, Large Soup Pot

6 Cups	Chicken Stock
1 T.	Soy Sauce
1 Large	Carrot, Sliced Fine on Diagonal
12	Snow Peas

·WONTONS·

½ Cup	Uncooked Chicken, Ground
½ Cup	Pork, Ground
1 tsp.	Soy Sauce
1 tsp.	Cornstarch
½ tsp.	Salt
½ T.	Carrot, Chopped Fine
1	Green Onion, Chopped Fine
24	Wonton Wrappers

Mix Wonton ingredients and place 1 tsp. in the center of each Wrapper. Bring up the edges of the Wrapper and press to seal. Set on a lightly oiled Baking Sheet until ready to use. Boil the Chicken Stock, Soy Sauce and Carrot for 5 Minutes. Add Wontons and cook 6 minutes. Add Peas and cook 3 Minutes or until Wontons are thoroughly cooked.

Variation: Add other Vegetables such as Baby Corn or Broccoli.

Hot Foods

Hamburger Basil Soup

This soup is easy to prepare and has become a family favorite. It has lots of flavor which you can heat up by adding more Red Pepper Sauce. I like to used different shaped pastas to give it variety.

Stove Top Required, Large Soup Pot, Yields 4-6 Servings

6 Cups	Beef Soup Stock
2 Large	Tomatoes, Diced
2 tsp.	Basil
2 tsp.	Oregano
$\frac{1}{2}$ tsp.	Salt
$\frac{1}{2}$ tsp.	Pepper
$\frac{1}{2}$ Cup	Ground Beef, Cooked
2 Med.	Onions, Chopped
$\frac{3}{4}$ Cup	Macaroni
$\frac{1}{4}$ Cup	Parmesan Cheese
3 Drops	Hot Pepper Sauce

Bring stock to a boil. Add Tomatoes, Spices, Hamburger and Onions. Simmer for 20 Minutes. Add the Macaroni, Cheese and Pepper Sauce. Cook until the Macaroni is tender. Serve.

Hot Foods

Minestrone Medley

A rich, nourishing soup full of beans, vegetables and pasta. Hearty and economical to make. What more could you ask of a soup? Add a Dash of Hot Pepper Sauce to spice it up.

Stove Top Required, Large Soup Pot

Hot Foods

6 Cups	Chicken Stock
1 Large	Onion
1 Large	Carrot, Diced
2	Celery Stalks, Diced
2 Large	Tomatoes, Diced
1 Small	Zucchini, Diced
1 Med.	Potato, Peeled and Diced
2 Cloves	Garlic, Diced
1 tsp.	Oregano
1 tsp.	Basil
2	Bay Leaf
	Salt & Pepper to Taste
1 Can	Kidney Beans or Chick Peas, Drained
¾ Cup	Small Pasta, Macaroni or Spiral
¼ Cup	Parmesan Cheese

Bring Stock to a Boil. Add Vegetables and Spices. Cook 10 Minutes. Add Kidney Beans and Pasta and cook until Pasta is tender. Season with Salt and Pepper to taste. Serve sprinkled with Parmesan Cheese.

Stove Top Baked Beans

My mom grows the most wonderful garden and baking beans is one of her specialties. I always look forward to the bag she gives me each fall. When I was young, baking beans were my favorite vegetable to harvest because it was the end of the season and we were allowed to pull up the whole plant to pick the beans off; unlike peas where we had to be careful not to damage the plant so we could get a second picking. Maybe it also had something to do with the fact that I loved baked beans and hated peas. I couldn't imagine why I should have to go to all the work of picking, shelling and freezing them when I didn't eat them. Kids will think of anything to get out of work.

Stove Top Required, Large Soup Pot

1 Cup	Baking Beans
7 Cups	Water
1	Ham Bone
$\frac{1}{2}$ Cup	Onion, Minced
1 tsp.	Brown Sugar
	Salt & Pepper to taste
2	Bay Leaves

Rinse Beans. Cover with Water and gently boil for 2 Min. Let stand, covered for 1 Hour. Drain and add Fresh Water. Add remaining ingredients and bring to a boil. Reduce to simmer and cook for 2 Hours. Bake in oven 30 Min. at 375°, if desired.

Mouthwatering Meatloaf

Hearty and satisfying, meatloaf can be served as a main dish or sliced and used as a sandwich filling.

Loaf Pan 9"X5", Bake 350° for 1 Hr. and 10 Min.

1 LB.	Ground Beef
1¼ Cups	Oatmeal, Uncooked
½ tsp.	Celery Salt
½ tsp.	Pepper
½ Cup	Milk
1 Large	Tomato, Chopped fine
1 Med.	Onion, Minced
1	Egg, Beaten
¼ Cup	Grated Cheese

Combine above ingredients thoroughly and pack into a greased loaf pan. Bake until done.

Easy Cheesy Macaroni

Cheesy, Creamy and Gooey, just like kids love it. Except the kids, like one of mine, who love to eat their pasta "just plain, please". I always cook extra pasta and set it aside for her before I mix in the rest of the ingredients. Talk about a calorie reduced meal. She wins that one.

Stove Top Required, Greased 9" X 9" Baking Dish
Bake at 350° for 30-40 Min.

$1\frac{1}{2}$ Cups	Macaroni or other Pasta, Cooked
2 T.	Butter, melted
2 T.	Flour
1 Cup	Milk
1 Cup	Grated Cheddar Cheese
	Salt and Pepper to taste

In a Sauce Pan, combine Butter and Flour. Add Milk slowly and whisk to prevent lumps. Boil to thicken, stirring constantly. Turn heat down and cook for 2 Min. Remove from heat. Add $\frac{1}{2}$ Cup of the Cheese and Salt and Pepper to taste. Stir to melt cheese and blend. Combine Macaroni and Sauce and put in a greased casserole. Sprinkle $\frac{1}{2}$ Cup of Cheese over top. If desired, sprinkle with crushed Soda Crackers.

Love It Lasagne

Lasagne is one of our kid's favorite meals. I like to serve it with a Lettuce, Caesar or Marinated Salad and Homemade Bread. Add a fresh fruit dessert and it's an eye appealing and hunger satisfying meal.

9" X 13" Baking Dish, Bake 350° for 45 Minutes

1 LB.	Ground Beef, Cooked (500g)
1 Med.	Onion, Finely Chopped
2 Med.	Tomatoes, Diced
1 14 oz.	Can Stewed Tomatoes (398 ml)
2 tsp.	Oregano
1	Egg, Optional
1 Cup	Cottage Cheese, Optional
¼ Cup	Parmesan Cheese, Optional
¾ LB.	Mozzarella Cheese, Shredded (350g)
	Lasagne Noodles, Cooked and Cooled
	Salt and Pepper to taste

Brown the Ground Beef. Add the Onion and Fresh Tomato and cook 5 Minutes. Add Oregano and Canned Tomatoes and simmer for 15 Minutes. Combine the Egg and Cottage Cheese. Omit them it you don't wish to use them. Put a layer of Lasagne Noodles in the Baking Dish. Add a layer of Meat Sauce and Shredded Cheese. Add ½ of the Egg Mixture. Repeat layers. Top with one more layer of Noodles, Meat and Cheese. Sprinkle with Parmesan Cheese. Bake covered for 30 Minutes. Uncover and continue baking 15 Minutes or until top is nicely browned. Stand 10 Minutes before serving. Freezes well.

Sandwiches

Sandwiches are a staple of packed lunches because they are easy to prepare and travel well. There are so many varieties of breads and fillings that if you mix and match them you'll have lots of fresh ideas for sandwiches.

BREADS	FILLINGS
White Bread	Jams and Jellies
Whole Wheat Bread	Peanut Butter
Rolls	Peanut Butter and Jelly
Dinner Buns	Cheese and Lettuce
Hot Cross Buns	Pizza Sauce and Cheese
Multi-Grain Breads	Peanut Butter, Honey, Banana
Crackers and Rice Cakes	Egg Salad, Cheese and Bacon Bits
Pretzels	Grilled Cheese
Tacos and Tortillas	Meat Loaf
Bagels	Cream Cheese, Raisins, Celery, Nuts
Biscuits	Tuna or Salmon
Muffins	Sliced Roasted Meats
Scones	Deli Meats
Hot Dog/Hamburger Buns	Cheese and Pickle
Baguettes	Apple, Cinnamon, Brown Sugar
Pitas	Apple and Cheese
Croissants	Nuts, Seeds, Raw Vegetables
Submarine Buns	Applesauce and Cinnamon

Pita Pocket Filling

*Pitas are a nice alternative to ordinary bread. You can buy
them but homemade ones are my favorite. I've included the
recipe in the Breads section. Fillings are limited only by your
imagination. Here's one your kids might love. Then again .... if
they don't love it this week, they might next. With kids and
food, you just never know.*

1 Med.	Carrot, Grated
1 Stalk	Celery, Chopped
	Raisins
	Chopped Dates
½ Cup	Peanut Butter or Cream Cheese

Prepare and mix ingredients. Spread a small amount in each
Pita Pocket.

Hard Boiled Egg Surprise

3	Eggs, Hard Boiled
1 tsp.	Onion, Minced
2 T.	Mayonnaise
½ tsp.	Mustard
	Salt & Pepper to taste
¼ Cup	Grated Cheese

Slice eggs in half lengthwise. Remove Yolks. Mash Yolks and
add above ingredients. Mix well and spoon back into Egg White
Halves. Garnish with Paprika, if desired. Put two halves
together to pack in lunches.

Sandwiches

Tuna Salad

My kids refuse to take tuna or salmon sandwiches in their lunch because of the smell. It can be a little overwhelming to be in a classroom when 20 or more lunchkits are opened all at once. I go along with their request and save fish for at home lunches. My experience as a parent has taught me that there are more important issues than food to be firm about.

1 Can	Tuna in Water, Drained
1 Stalk	Celery, Diced
1	Green Onion, Diced
3 T.	Plain Yogurt
1 T.	Mayonnaise

Serve in Pita Pockets or Ice Cream Cones topped with a Radish or Cherry Tomato. Other things you can add to Tuna Sandwiches include: slices of Tomato, Onion, Green Pepper, Cucumber, Pickle, Sweet Relish, Shredded Lettuce, Grated Carrot, Grated Cheese or Sliced Egg.

Sandwiches

Tuna Melt

For a tasty at home lunch, mix drained Tuna with 2 T. Chopped Sweet Pickle, Chopped Celery, Diced Onion, Grated Cheese and 3 T. Mayonnaise. Place under the broiler until lightly browned and the Cheese melts. Or, slice a Bread Loaf lengthwise, spread with the filling, wrap in foil and bake for 5 Min. at 400°.

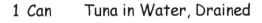

Turkey or Chicken Salad

Leftover turkey and chicken takes on a new life when mixed with a few ingredients to make a tasty sandwich filling.

2 Cups	Cooked Turkey or Chicken, Diced
½ Cup	Celery, Diced
¼ Cup	Onion, Minced
2	Hard Boiled Eggs
1 T.	Lemon Juice
	Salt and Pepper to Taste
½ Cup	Mayonnaise
Dash	Cayenne Pepper

Mix well. Refrigerate for several hours so flavors are well blended before serving.

Homemade Gee Whiz

My friend, Janine gave me the recipe for this smooth and creamy spread. It can be used on sandwiches, vegetables such as celery, or heat and pour over pasta.

½ T.	Flour
1 T.	Butter
9 Oz.	Milk
3 Cups	Cubed Cheddar Cheese

Put all ingredients in a blender and process on High until smooth and creamy. This takes about 6 minutes. Store in fridge.

Sandwiches

Desserts

Dessert may not contribute a lot of nutrition to a bag lunch but it adds contrast and appeal. Remember, moderation in all things and you'll keep dessert in perspective. Desserts are usually high in fat and sugar so to justify making them, I like to use recipes that have some added nutrition in the form of whole grains, oatmeal, nuts, coconut and fruits. We have a joke at our house that you can only eat three cookies at a time so the bigger you make them the better. If you serve cookies as a snack, include a glass of milk and some fresh fruit or vegetables to make the snack more nutritious.

Chocolate Pecan Turtles

These are so easy to make and taste delicious. I like to make them for Christmas. To keep them from being eaten too quickly, I hide them in the freezer in a container marked spinach. Get your kids to help make them.

Stove Top Required, Wax Paper Lined Cookie Sheet, Yields 60

120	Pecan Halves
1 Can	Sweetened Condensed Milk (300 ml)
1½ Cups	Milk Chocolate Chips

Put Sweetened Condensed Milk into a Pint Jar. Put jar lid on loosely and set in a pan of boiling water. Cover pot and simmer for 3 hours until the Condensed Milk caramelizes. Check to make sure it doesn't boil dry. Place 2 Pecan halves side by side on the cookie sheet. Put a tsp. of the Caramel Sauce on each pair of Pecans. Melt the Chocolate Chips and coat the top of each Turtle with chocolate. Cool in fridge.

Desserts

Egg Shell Chocolate Chip Bars

This cookie tastes much better than it sounds. It got it's name because I was baking in a big rush with a new baby needing to be fed. After the bars were baked, I discovered that half an eggshell had been mixed into the batter. We could pick out the big pieces but the smaller ones were a little crunchy. We all got our calcium requirement for the week and a good laugh. This versatile dough can be baked as individual cookies or spread out on a cookie sheet and cut into squares after it's baked.

Bake Bars 350° F. 18-20 Min., Bake Cookies 350° F. 8-10 Min.

½ Cup	Butter
½ Cup	Oil
1 Cup	White Sugar
½ Cup	Brown Sugar
2	Eggs
2 tsp.	Vanilla
¼ tsp.	Salt
1 tsp.	Baking Soda
1½ Cups	Flour
½ Cup	Oatmeal
1 Cup	Favorite Nuts, Optional
1½ Cups	Chocolate Chips

Mix ingredients in order given. To make bars, spread dough evenly on a 10" X 15" Cookie Sheet. To make cookies, drop by spoonful onto a cookie sheet.

Cowboy Cookies

Everyone seems to be baking cowboy cookies these days. If you haven't found a great recipe yet, try this one. You can cut the recipe in half if you want a smaller batch. I make the large batch and freeze half of the dough either in a large container or rolled into cookie size logs. I use a melon baller to scoop the dough out of the container while it is still frozen. If I have taken time to roll the logs, they are easy to cut into slices when slightly thawed and make nice round cookies when baked. Using one of these methods, I can quickly cook a pan of fresh cookies along with an oven meal.

Bake Cookies 350° F. for 8-10 Minutes

1 Cup	Butter
1 Cup	Oil
2 Cups	White Sugar
2 Cups	Brown Sugar
4	Eggs
1 T.	Vanilla
1 tsp.	Salt
2 tsp.	Baking Soda
1 tsp.	Baking Powder
4 Cups	Flour
4 Cups	Oatmeal
1½ Cups	Milk Chocolate Chips

Cream Butter, Oil and Sugars. Add Eggs and beat until light and fluffy. Add remaining ingredients and mix until well blended. Drop by spoonful onto cookie sheets.

Fortune Cookies

Making your own fortune cookies takes a little work but it's lots of fun to write little messages to put inside them and they look so appealing when they are all folded and laid out on a plate. Children could help write the messages and mix the batter. You will need about 20 messages written on clean paper strips cut to 3" X ½". "Be careful when folding the hot cookies so you don't burn your fingers," warns my oldest daughter as she immerses her fingers in cold water. After all that advice, I still hope you'll try making your own. It really is worth it.

Bake Cookies at 400° F. for 3-5 Minutes, Greased Cookie Sheet

---

2		Egg Whites
¼	Cup	Butter, Melted
½	Cup	Sugar
½	Cup	Flour
2	tsp.	Water
½	tsp.	Vanilla

Whisk the Egg Whites, Sugar, Flour, Melted Butter, Water and Vanilla until well blended. Drop by rounded teaspoon onto a greased baking sheet. Use the back of the spoon to spread the batter into a 3" circle. Bake 3 to 4 cookies at a time until edges are lightly browned. Remove from oven. Quickly loosen cookies and turn over. Place message in the center and fold over in half. Bring ends around, bending the folded edge of the cookie back over the rim of a glass to form a traditional fortune cookie shape. Place in a muffin tin to hold the shape until cooled. Work quickly before cookies have time to cool. If you didn't get them folded quickly enough, you can put them back in the oven just until reheated and softened. Spread the batter thinly and evenly to make them easier to fold. **Variation:** Use frozen fruit juice concentrate such as grape or raspberry in place of the water to make colorful cookies with a change of flavor.

Dessert Taco Cookies

Make 4½" circles with this batter. Bake. Remove from oven and drape over an empty paper towel roll or some similar shaped item, that has been covered with wax paper. Allow to cool completely. This will form the cookie into a taco shape which can be filled with ice cream or sherbet, fresh fruit and whipped cream.

Raspberry Swirl Coconut Cookies

This is a chewy cookie that looks appealing with it's raspberry jam center.

Bake Cookies 350° F. for 10-12 Minutes.

$\frac{1}{2}$	Cup	Butter
$\frac{1}{2}$	Cup	Oil
1	Cup	Brown Sugar
$\frac{3}{4}$	Cup	White Sugar
2		Eggs
1	tsp.	Baking Soda
$\frac{1}{2}$	tsp.	Salt
1	tsp.	Vanilla
$\frac{1}{2}$	Cup	Water
2	Cups	Flour
2	Cups	Oatmeal
2	Cups	Flake Coconut
		Raspberry Jam

Cream the Butter, Oil and Sugars. Add the eggs and beat until light and fluffy. Add the remaining ingredients except the Jam. Drop by spoonful unto ungreased cookie sheets. Make a small cavity in each cookie and fill with jam.

Desserts

Gingerbread

Since our kids were small, we have been getting together with friends to make Gingerbread Houses. Each child has a set of miniature Nativity Figures that were purchased at a Craft Store. We use the gingerbread to build a stable for each child. There's always some left over from this batch to make cookie cutouts. I've included a pattern for an A-frame gingerbread house that is much easier to construct than the traditional house style. This gingerbread recipe came from my sister-in-law, Karen. It's so good, it's the only one I use.

Bake Cookies 350° F. for 8-10 Minutes.
Bake the gingerbread pieces for a house 10-12 Minutes. It's usually best to bake it the night before so it is dry and hard for decorating.

1 Cup	Butter
1 Cup	White Sugar
1 Cup	Molasses
1 Cup	Milk mixed with 1 tsp. Vinegar
4	Eggs
3 tsp.	Baking Soda
½ tsp.	Salt
1 tsp.	Ginger
2 tsp.	Cinnamon
½ tsp.	Cloves
½ tsp.	Nutmeg
	Flour

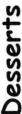

Mix in the order given, adding enough flour to make a soft dough that will roll easily. Roll on a floured counter and cut into desired shapes.

Desserts

Gingerbread A-Frame House

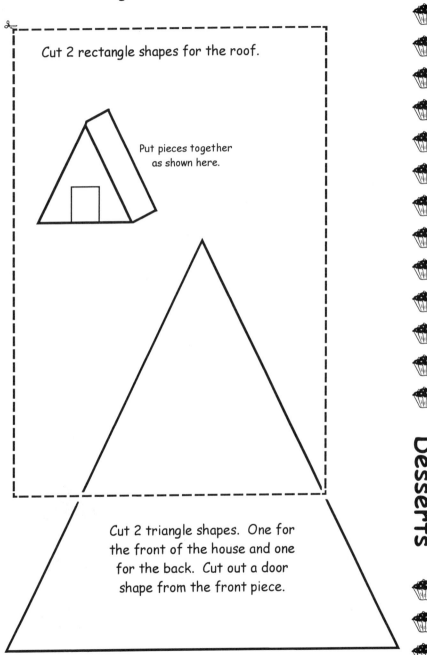

Cut 2 rectangle shapes for the roof.

Put pieces together as shown here.

Cut 2 triangle shapes. One for the front of the house and one for the back. Cut out a door shape from the front piece.

Desserts

Crispy Rice Shapes

This traditional recipe is usually pressed into a cake pan and cut into squares. It's very moldable when warm and can be used in a number of other ways.

- *Add green Food coloring and form into cone tree shapes. Shake on cake sprinkles and use gumdrops to decorate.*
- *Add red food coloring and press into a cookie mold to make heart shapes. Decorate with heart shaped candies.*
- *Roll 2 balls of decreasing size, roll in coconut, stack and decorate as snowmen.*
- *Press into a muffin tin to make a crust to hold fresh fruit.*
- *Press into a pie plate. Add a layer of pudding, a layer of fresh fruit and top with whip cream.*

Stove Top required. No Baking required
1 - greased 13" X 9" Pan

¼ Cup	Butter
5 Cups	Miniature Marshmallows
½ tsp.	Vanilla
6 Cups	Crisp Rice Cereal

Melt the butter in a large saucepan over low heat. Add the marshmallows and stir until melted. Remove from heat and add the vanilla and cereal. Mix well. Using a lightly buttered spatula, press into a buttered 13" X 9" pan or form some of the special shapes described above.

TREE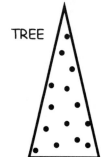

HEART

SNOWMAN

Puffed Cereal Bars

These chocolate coated cereal bars can be pressed into a pan and cut into bars or pressed into muffin tins to make individual servings which can be frozen for later use.

Stove Top required. No Baking required.
1 - greased 13" X 9" Pan

½ Cup	Brown Sugar
⅓ Cup	Corn Syrup
2 T.	Cocoa
½ Cup	Butter

Boil for 3 minutes over medium heat. Stir constantly to avoid burning. Remove from heat and add Vanilla

1 tsp.	Vanilla
8 Cups	Puffed Wheat Cereal

Add the Puffed Wheat Cereal and mix well. Press into a greased pan and allow to cool.

Variations: Use Puffed Rice Cereal or a combination of Puffed Wheat and Rice. To make individual servings, use muffin tins for the pan or press the mixture into balls and allow to cool on wax paper. You could also press the mixture into plastic molds or a bundt pan.

Desserts

Oatmeal Cinnamon Swirl Quick Loaf

This loaf bread really is quick to make and serves up great hot from the oven or cold. It also travels well in packed lunches.

Bake Loaves 350° F. for 45-50 Minutes
2 - Greased 9"X5"X3" Loaf Pans

½	Cup	Oil
1½	Cups	White Sugar
2	tsp.	Baking Soda
1	tsp.	Salt
1	tsp.	Vanilla
2	Cups	Buttermilk

· TOPPING·

¼	Cup	Melted Butter
¼	Cup	Brown Sugar
1	Cup	Rolled Oats
¼	tsp.	Oatmeal
1½	tsp.	Cinnamon

Cream Butter, Sugar and Eggs until light and fluffy. Add remaining ingredients and mix until well blended. Mix Topping ingredients. Fill each pan with ¼ of the batter and top with ¼ of the topping. Add the remaining batter to the pans and top with the remaining topping. Swirl a knife through the batter. Cool 10 minutes before removing from the pans.

Barley Banana Loaf

This loaf bread is a great way to use up over-ripe bananas. The barley adds an appealing flavor.

Bake Loaves 350° F. for 50-60 Minutes
1 - Greased 9"X5"X3" Loaf Pan

$\frac{1}{4}$ Cup	Oil
$\frac{3}{4}$ Cup	Brown Sugar
2	Eggs
1 Cup	Mashed Banana (about 3 medium)
1 tsp.	Baking Powder
1 tsp.	Baking Soda
$\frac{1}{2}$ tsp.	Salt
$\frac{1}{4}$ tsp.	Nutmeg
2 Cups	Barley Flour
$\frac{1}{4}$ Cup	Milk
$\frac{1}{2}$ Cup	Chopped Nuts

Cream Butter, Sugar, Eggs and Banana until light and fluffy. Add remaining ingredients. Bake in loaf pan. Cool 10 minutes before removing from the pan.

Desserts

Chocoluscious Cake

Chocolate cake has always been my favorite. This recipe comes from my mom. She always bakes chocolate cake for us when we go to visit. Chocolate Cake with Chocolate Icing in a bowl of Mom's home canned peaches. That's my favorite dessert. This recipe can be baked in one large pan, divided among 3 round pans or baked as cupcakes.

> Bake in a Greased 13" x 9" Pan for 35-40 Min. at 350° F.
> Bake in 3 - Greased 8" Pans for 25-30 Min. at 350° F.
> Bake Cupcakes for 20-25 Min. at 350° F.

½ Cup	Cocoa
½ Cup	Boiling Water

Blend Cocoa and Boiling Water.

⅔ Cup	Vegetable Oil
1 ¾ Cups	Sugar
2	Eggs
1 tsp.	Vanilla

Blend Oil, Sugar, Eggs and Vanilla. Add Cocoa mixture.

1½ tsp.	Baking Soda
½ tsp.	Salt
2¾ Cups	Flour
1 ⅓ Cups	Buttermilk (or mix 4 tsp. Vinegar and enough milk to make 1 1/3 Cups)

Add remaining ingredients and mix until well blended. Cool 10 minutes before removing from pans.

Desserts

Black Bottom Cupcakes

My family loves Black Bottom Cupcakes. The recipe for the Cream Cheese filling came from our friend, Linda. I use the Chocoluscious Cake recipe from the facing page to make these delicious cupcakes.

Bake cupcakes for 20-25 Min. at 350° F.	

1	Chocoluscious Cake Batter (see previous page)
1 Pkg.	Cream Cheese (8 oz./250 g)
1	Egg, slightly beaten
$\frac{1}{3}$ Cup	Sugar
1 tsp.	Vanilla
1 pkg.	Milk Chocolate Chips (6 oz./170 g)

Prepare the Chocoluscious Cake batter and fill paper lined muffin cups, 3/4 full. Combine the Cream Cheese, Egg, Sugar and Vanilla until smooth and creamy. Add Chocolate Chips. Place a spoonful of the Cream Cheese mixture on top of each of the cupcakes. Makes 24+ cupcakes.

Variation: Bake in flat bottomed ice cream cones set in muffin cups. Fill the cones to within $\frac{1}{2}$" of the top. Add Cream Cheese Topping before baking, if desired. Bake at 325° F. for 30-35 Minutes. If you bake plain cone cakes, ice with your favorite icing, dip in Candy Sprinkles and top off with a Cherry.

Desserts

Royal Raspberry Cake

This cake is great served warm with ice cream and also travels well in lunches. My kids love it and even eat it for breakfast, if they can get away with having dessert for breakfast. My sister-in-law, Janet gave this "quick to prepare" recipe to me.

$\frac{1}{3}$	Cup	Oil (or Butter)
$\frac{3}{4}$	Cup	Sugar
1		Egg, at room temperature
1	T.	Baking Powder
$\frac{1}{2}$	tsp.	Salt
1	tsp.	Vanilla
1		Cup Milk
2	Cups	Flour
$3\frac{1}{2}$	Cups	Fresh or Frozen Raspberries

•Glaze•

$1\frac{1}{2}$	Cups	Icing Sugar
2	T.	Cream
1	T.	Butter
1	tsp.	Vanilla

Desserts

Blend Oil, Sugar and Egg. Add remaining ingredients, except fruit and blend well. Pour batter into pan. Spread Berries evenly over top. Bake. Cool 5 minutes. Mix glaze ingredients and drizzle over Berries.

Pumpkin Chocolate Chip Muffins

If your kids don't think they like pumpkin, this is a good way to disguise it. These muffins can also be made with over-ripe bananas.

Bake in Greased Muffin Tins for 18-20 Min. at 400° F. Yields 12

$1\frac{1}{2}$	Cups	Flour
3	tsp.	Baking Powder
$\frac{1}{2}$	tsp	Salt
$\frac{1}{2}$	tsp.	Cinnamon
$\frac{1}{4}$	tsp.	Nutmeg
$\frac{1}{2}$	Cup	Brown Sugar
1		Egg
$\frac{1}{4}$	Cup	Oil
$\frac{3}{4}$	Cup	Milk
$\frac{2}{3}$	Cup	Milk Chocolate Chips
$\frac{1}{2}$	Cup	Pumpkin Puree

Blend all ingredients and pour into muffin tins. Bake.

Variations:
1. Use Pureed Banana in place of the Pumpkin.

2. Use $1\frac{1}{2}$ Cups finely grated Carrot and $\frac{1}{2}$ Cup Raisins in place of the Pumpkin and Chips.

3. Use $1\frac{1}{2}$ Cups finely chopped Apple and $\frac{1}{2}$ Cup Raisins in place of the Pumpkin and Chips. Mix 2 T. Sugar with $\frac{1}{4}$ tsp. Cinnamon and sprinkle over tops before baking.

Blueberry Oatmeal Muffins

Busy Parents usually don't have much time for baking, so I love recipes that you can throw all the ingredients in a bowl and mix in a hurry. This recipe works well with this method, making it easy to whip up a batch to go with a meal or pack in lunches. This recipe is based on one from my Sister-in-law, Evelyn. It doubles well for a larger batch. I usually divide a double batch in half and use the variations given below to make 2 kinds of muffins.

Bake in Greased Muffin Tins 18-20 Min. at 400° F. Yields 12

¼ Cup	Oil
1	Egg
½ Cup	Brown Sugar
1 tsp.	Baking Powder
½ tsp.	Baking Soda
½ tsp.	Salt
1¼ Cups	Flour
1 Cup	Sour Milk (Add 1 tsp. Vinegar to enough Milk to make 1 Cup)
1 Cup	Oatmeal
1 Cup	Blueberries (Fresh or Frozen)

Mix all ingredients except the Blueberries until just combined. Add Blueberries. Stir lightly and pour into muffin tins. Bake.

Variations: 1. Mix 2 T. of Sugar with ¼ tsp. Cinnamon and sprinkle over tops before baking.

2. Replace Blueberries with 1 Cup Choc. Chips

3. Replace Blueberries with chopped Cherries.

Desserts

Double Strawberry Pie

This dessert tastes best made from freshly picked strawberries but frozen berries can also be used. To freeze fresh berries, I spread the berries out on cookie trays. When frozen, I put them in large bags. This way the berries do not freeze together and I can easily scoop the amount I need out of the bag.

---

1 Baked 9" Pie Shell. Stove Top Required.

Crush

1 Cup	Fresh or Frozen Strawberries

Add

1 Cup	Water
½ Cup	Sugar
3 T.	Cornstarch

Cook over Medium Heat until thick and bubbly.

3 Cups	Fresh or Frozen Strawberries

Place 3 Cups of Strawberries in a cooked pie shell. Pour the cooked strawberries over them and chill. Serve with whipped cream topping.

This dessert can be made in a pie plate or dish without a crust. If your kids just eat the filling and leave the crust, why bother with it. Put individual portions in plastic containers to send in lunches.

Variation: Substitute Blueberries for Strawberries.

139

Desserts

Applesauce

Applesauce also makes a great topping for pancakes.

Stove Top Required.

4	Apples
2 T.	Water
¼ tsp.	Cinnamon

Core, peel and quarter the Apples. Combine ingredients in a saucepan. Cover and cook over medium heat for 10 minutes, stirring occasionally.

Finger Jelly-O

Easy to make and fun to eat. Divide the recipe in half and use 2 different kinds of juice to make a layered effect. Add the second layer once the first one is firmly set.

Stove Top Required. 9" X 5" Loaf Pan

2 Pkgs.	Unflavored Gelatin (7 g each)
½ Cup	Water
3 Cups	Fruit Juice such as Grape, Apple, Pear, Raspberry or Combination.

Soften the Gelatin in the Water. Add ½ of the Fruit Juice and cook over low heat until the gelatin dissolves. Remove from heat and add remaining Juice. Pour into a lightly greased loaf pan. Refrigerate until firm, about 3 hours.

Desserts

Banana Pudding

Creamy Banana Pudding slides down so easily. You can turn this recipe into pie by pouring it into a Graham Cracker Crust and layering it with Banana slices. Top with Whipped Cream.

Stove Top Required.	

½ Cup	Sugar
2 T.	Cornstarch
2 T.	Flour
2	Eggs
2 Cups	Milk

Mix until thoroughly blended. Cook over medium heat until thickened, stirring constantly. Continue cooking for 2 minutes. Remove from heat.

2 T.	Butter
1 tsp.	Vanilla

Stir in Butter and Vanilla. Layer in individual containers with Banana slices or cut the Banana into chunks and stir right in.

Desserts

Butterscotch Pudding

This Butterscotch Pudding is also delicious when put in a pre-cooked Pie Shell or Graham Crust and topped with Whipped Cream.

---

1 Baked 9" Pie Shell. Stove Top Required.

---

1 Cup	Brown Sugar
2 T.	Corn Starch
3 T.	Flour
½ tsp.	Salt
2	Eggs

Mix above ingredients very thoroughly.

2 Cups	Warm Milk

Add the Milk and cook over medium heat, boiling for 3 minutes or until thickened. Remove from heat and add

2 T.	Butter
1 tsp.	Vanilla

Pour into a pie crust or dish and cover with plastic wrap to prevent a skin from forming as it cools.

Put into individual serving containers or pre-cooked Tart Shells to send in lunches.

Sensational Snacks

Busy, active children need fuel to keep their bodies healthy. If you teach your children to be aware of their body's needs, it will be easier for them to know when they need to fuel up. You should also make them aware of "external hunger triggers" such as T.V. commercials, watching others eat, reading about food, and smelling food. All of these can make you feel like eating when you really aren't hungry.

Depending on activity levels, children may require snacks in between regular meals. Snacks can be thought of as mini-meals. Being part of the overall daily food plan, they should provide foods from the 4 main food groups. Aim to provide snacks that give immediate satisfaction in taste, texture and visual appeal, and supply long term energy in the form of complex carbohydrates.

When my children were pre-schoolers, I offered snacks mid-morning and afternoon. I discouraged snacking close to bedtime. Consider each of your child's individual needs when choosing snack times.

The snacks in this section can be served between meals, after school or for school snack days. For more snack ideas, check out the **Fun Foods** in the **Perk It Up Section**.

Smore

*This is my backup when there are no cookies in the house.
That is, if no one has discovered my latest hiding spot for the
Chocolate Chips and Marshmallows. I used to raid my parent's
cupboards for Chocolate Chips and now I discovered my kids
love to eat them straight from the bag, too. Must be
hereditary.*

Microwave or Toaster Oven

Pile as many Chocolate Chips and Marshmallows, on a Square
Wheat Cracker, as possible. Microwave for 20 Seconds or put
in a toaster oven until melted. Top with a second Cracker.
Allow to cool and enjoy. For a different taste, add a layer of
Peanut Butter to the Cracker.

We have another version of Smores created by our middle
daughter, Cathryn. She calls it **Banana Smess**. To make it,
put Chocolate Chips and Marshmallows in a bowl and microwave.
Add a sliced Banana and stir. Eat with a spoon. Messy but
delicious.

Baked Pumpkin Seeds

Bake at 375° F. for 20 Min.

Wash Pumpkin Seeds thoroughly. Place on a cookie sheet and
bake, stirring occasionally. Remove, cool and eat.

Snacks

Cereal Surprise

Using a variety of cereals in this snack makes it more interesting. Use it as a topping for Yogurt for a change of pace.

Bake at 250° F. for 30-45 Min. Yields 6 Cups

$\frac{1}{3}$ Cup	Butter, Melted
4 tsp.	Worcestershire Sauce
1 tsp.	Seasoning Salt
1	Cup Pretzels
$\frac{3}{4}$ Cup	Nuts, Shelled
6 Cups	Dry Cereals,

Mix all ingredients thoroughly and place on a cookie sheet. Bake until crisp, stirring every 15 min. Remove from oven and blot on paper towels.

Carrot Curls and Celery Fans

To make delicious **Carrot Curls**, use a vegetable peeler to cut long slices off a Carrot. Soak the slices in ice water until crisp and curled.

To make **Celery Fans**, cut Celery into 6" pieces. Cut each piece in thin slices stopping 1" from the end of the Celery stick. Soak in cold water until the ends fan out.

Snacks

Fruit Leather

Making your own fruit leather is a great way to use extra fruit and gives you control over the ingredients.

Dry in Oven at 140° F. for 1-2 Hours with Oven Door Open 2"

| 2 Cups | Fruit |
| 1 tsp. | Lemon Juice |

2 T.   Sugar

Use fully ripe Fruit. Clean Fruit as necessary by washing, removing skin, pitting and chopping. Combine with the Sugar and Lemon Juice. Boil, reduce heat and simmer until Fruit is softened. Pureé in a food processor or blender. Line a cookie sheet with greased foil and pour pureé to a $\frac{1}{4}$" thickness. Dry in the oven until leathery and non-sticky. Store in fridge or freezer.

Wormy Dirt Delight

Fill a clear container or dish with Chocolate Pudding. Top with crushed Chocolate Wafers. Add Gummy Worms and serve. Delicious.

Snacks

Marinated Vegetables

A favorite way to serve raw vegetables. Use a variety of vegetables as the colors and shapes make the dish visually appealing.

Refrigeration Required

$\frac{1}{3}$ Cup	Salad Oil
$\frac{1}{3}$ Cup	Cider Vinegar
2 T.	Green Pepper, Chopped Fine
1 tsp.	Salt
$\frac{1}{4}$ tsp.	Pepper
$\frac{1}{4}$ tsp.	Paprika

Mix all ingredients thoroughly.

7 Cups	Mixed Raw Vegetables

Prepare Vegetables and cut into chunks. Pour Dressing over Vegetables and mix well. Cover and marinate in fridge for several hours or over night.

 ### Carrot Fluff

Serving an ordinary food in a different way can be a hit. For a school snack, I grated Carrots and gave each child a mound of Carrot, a handful of Raisins, small slices of Celery and Cucumber. Before eating, I encouraged them to create faces, using the grated Carrot for hair. Kids know that playing with food can make it taste better.

Snacks

Italian Dressing

*Use this dressing on a lettuce salad or substitute in the
Marinated Vegetable recipe on the previous page.*

Refrigeration Required

$\frac{1}{3}$	Cup	Vegetable Oil
$\frac{1}{3}$	Cup	Vinegar
2		Green Onion, Minced
$\frac{1}{2}$	tsp.	Salt
$\frac{1}{4}$	tsp.	Pepper
$\frac{1}{2}$	tsp.	Dry Mustard
$\frac{1}{2}$	tsp.	Basil

Mix all ingredients thoroughly.

Sandwich Cookies

If I have a little Icing left over, I use it to make Sandwich
Cookies. My mom used to give us this in our lunches when she
ran out of cookies. I thought they were delicious.

Layer 3 plain Cookies or Graham Wafers together with Jelly in
between one layer and Icing between the other. Wrap. The
Cookies soften by lunch time and taste yummy.

Snacks

Baked Potato Chips

Easy to make and delicious. I grew up eating raw potato and am always surprised when people have never heard of eating uncooked potato. My family loves raw potato and it's rare to get them all peeled without hearing, "Piece of Potato, please."

Bake at 450° F. for 10 Minutes

Use a knife or Food Slicer to thinly slice Potatoes. Soak in ice water in the refrigerator for 30 Minutes. Place on a non-stick or lightly greased cookie sheet. If desired, sprinkle lightly with Salt or other Spices before baking. Bake until crispy, turning when half done.

Apple Surprise

Have you ever cut an Apple in half through the middle instead of end to end? If not, you and your children will be surprised to discover that the seed cases form a star when cut in this direction. For a change of pace, I slice the whole Apple this way and the kids eat around the star.

Litterless Snack

When children want to take a snack outdoors to eat, serve it in a flat bottom Ice Cream Cone. The children can eat the snack and the cone and there's no mess to throw away.

Savory Salsa

This recipe came from my sister, Shirley who got it from our cousin, Brenda. Anyone who tries it always wants the recipe. It's easy to make but "remember to wear rubber gloves when you cut the peppers or you'll be soaking your hands in cold water for hours". That's my sister's voice of experience speaking. Salsa should be canned, or refrigerated and used within a short period of time.

Large Sauce Pan, 6 Pint Jars
Can Using Hot Water Bath, Process 15 Minutes

---

5 LBS.	Tomatoes (4 litres)
3 Cups	Onions, Chopped
1 Cup	Chili (Jalepeno) Pepper, Seeded and Chopped
1 Cup	Cider Vinegar (5% Acidity)
$3\frac{1}{2}$ tsp.	Salt
3 Cloves	Garlic, Crushed

Skin and chop Tomatoes. Combine with remaining ingredients and bring to a boil, stirring often. Reduce heat and simmer for 30 Minutes or until desired consistency. Immediately fill prepared jars and process for 15 Minutes.

Snacks

A Final Word

When you consider how many lunches each child will eat during their school years, it's not surprising that we run out of ideas and motivation. Super Easy Bag Lunches was written to share ideas and inspire you to make creative bag lunches. Getting your children actively involved in the planning and preparation of lunches gives them an opportunity to take responsibility and make decisions while learning life skills. With a little effort and imagination, a routine chore can be turned into an enjoyable experience for your whole family.

LUNCH LAUGHS

Have you ever made a lunch goof?

·Our middle daughter still talks about the time she was looking forward to eating left over pizza in her lunch. When she opened the container, she was disappointed to find soggy spaghetti, instead. I had unfortunately grabbed the wrong container when I hurriedly packed her lunch.

·A friend shared that her husband was eating lunch with his co-workers and got a surprise when he bit into his sandwich and she had forgotten to remove the plastic wrap from the cheese slice. With a laugh, he commented, "That's my wife. I think I'll keep her."

·When our niece, Jacqueline was small she liked to flatten her sandwiches before eating them. Her dad certainly got a surprise one day when she made his lunch and pre-flattened his sandwiches for him.

It's Your Turn

We'd love to hear from you. If you have questions, comments, suggestions, ideas, recipes, lunch notes or funny lunch stories you would like to share, write it here and mail to us at the address below.
Please include your name and address.

_____

_____

_____

_____

_____

_____

_____

_____

_____

_____

_____

_____

_____

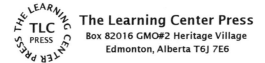

The Learning Center Press
Box 82016 GMO#2 Heritage Village
Edmonton, Alberta T6J 7E6

Index

Index

SUPER EASY
BAG LUNCHES

is available in bookstores or by mail. **To order by mail**,
complete the order form and send to the address below.
Super Easy Bag Lunches can be mailed to your address or
purchased for gifts and mailed directly to the recipient's
address. Please indicate your address and the address you wish
the books to be mailed to. To use this book as a **fund raiser**
for your group, write for an information package.

ORDER FORM FOR SUPER EASY BAG LUNCHES

_____ Copies @ $16.95	$_____
Postage and Handling	$___N/C___
G.S.T. 7% Canadian Orders	$_____
Total Order	$_____

☐ Cheque or ☐ Money Order Enclosed
Payable to: The Learning Center Press

MY ADDRESS

NAME _____

ADDRESS _____

_____

SHIP TO ■ MY ADDRESS OR ■ FOLLOWING ADDRESS

NAME _____

ADDRESS _____

_____

The Learning Center Press
Box 82016 GMO#2 Heritage Village
Edmonton, Alberta T6J 7E6

SUPER EASY
BAG LUNCHES

GREAT FOR GIFTS
& FUND RAISERS

is available in bookstores or by mail. **To order by mail,**
complete the order form and send to the address below.
Super Easy Bag Lunches can be mailed to your address or
purchased for gifts and mailed directly to the recipient's
address. Please indicate your address and the address you wish
the books to be mailed to. To use this book as a **fund raiser**
for your group, write for an information package.

ORDER FORM FOR SUPER EASY BAG LUNCHES

_____ Copies @ $16.95 $_____

Postage and Handling $___N/C____

G.S.T. 7% Canadian Orders $_____

Total Order $_____

☐ Cheque or ☐ Money Order Enclosed
Payable to: The Learning Center Press

MY ADDRESS
NAME _____

ADDRESS _____

_____

SHIP TO ■ MY ADDRESS OR ■ FOLLOWING ADDRESS
NAME _____

ADDRESS _____

_____

TLC
PRESS

The Learning Center Press
Box 82016 GMO#2 Heritage Village
Edmonton, Alberta T6J 7E6